ORIGINAL DIAMOND BOY 2

Against All Odds

LE'TAXIONE®

WORKS BY LE'TAXIONE®

Gang Violence Prevention Curricula:
Nine Steps to Empowerment Process Gang Violence Prevention and Intervention Curriculum
Gangology 101: The New Paradigm (N'STEP©'s 2nd Edition)

Memoires:
Original Diamond Boy: The Psychology of a Gangbanger
Original Diamond Boy 2: Against All Odds

Children's Books:
I Am More Than a Gang Member
A Bully's Behavior
I Love Myself

Urban Fiction:
Street Poisoned
Nobody Cries

Novels:
Concrete Roses

Coming Soon:
The Psychodynamics of the Gang Mentality
Administrative Lynching
Still Breathing
The Silence of a Cell
30 Pieces of Silver
Mary
Gangology 2.0: The New Paradigm

Dedication

I dedicate Original Diamond Boy 2: Against All Odds to all of the Structural Gang Culture© members who languish behind the steel curtains of the prison industrial complex.

I overstand the demonstration and the adversity that you face on a continuum. At the same time, realize that we place ourselves at the mercy of the judicial system that has historically been discriminative in its application of the law concerning the poor, miseducated, and impoverished.

It is the violence that we perpetuate in our communities that subjects us to legislation that results in the mass incarceration of our comrades; and once incarceration is actualized, we face the degradation and dehumanization superimposed upon us through a capricious penological ideology, which in turn cultivates recidivism.

It is time that we identify the psychological and sociological trauma that we were exposed to – as the culprits that made violence and the lure of the streets so attractive that we are willing to live and die for those miniscule trappings in our "quest for relevance". For in this introspection lies life, liberation, and success for us in our communities.

Le'Taxione®

Introduction

While on duty within an organization of social justice and change aimed at educating inmates within the American prison industrial complex – I came across Le'Taxione®'s name and work. I was shocked that I had never seen his work before. It had nothing to do with my living in Canada, or not being familiar with inmate advocacy and education – I had already gained experience in such campaigns and was aware if the mandates of popular organizations. But not aware of Le'Taxione®'s work – this was a disappointment. I had been present at board meetings of various groups. I had been present in department meetings organizing and creating curriculums and educational materials -seemingly conducting research and development.

Le'Taxione® had already accomplished a corpus of work in this regard – based on multiple sciences – addressing a marginalized section of society – present in communities nationwide – who are losing their battle – on their way to the prison yard or the graveyard.

Who was preventing his work from reaching the people who need it the most? None of it made sense then – but it does now. Not all organizations of social justice and change are genuinely working on behalf of our communities. Not all campaigns regarding advocacy and public awareness are of added value to the people. They exhibit form over functionality – in disarray with poor organizational structure. Some of our boards stagnate in rhetoric and nostalgia while families bury their loved ones.

Let me be pellucid. We have within the Struggle – individuals who purport to be committed to mental and physical liberation – who deter progress as the means of maintaining their relevance in society. There are mascots and mannequins – disguised as advocates – in front of media cameras cutting ribbons and posing at vigils – who consciously make no advancement on behalf of the people – as the downtrodden provide these individuals with income -status – resources – even prayers – to no avail. Our suffering is their meal.

The arrogance of the status quo will cost more lives -frustrate the struggle – hide the truth – punish the honorable – reward sophistry and subterfuge – appoint misleaders – create more opportunities of oppression – while smiling at us before slithering off to their meetings and venues of political and socio-economical tactics.

Those who have careers within the prison industrial complex who have chosen to dehumanize themselves and become agents of human and societal destruction – will recognize pieces of their demonstration in Original Diamond Boy 2. Le'Taxione® has championed you and will continue to do so. You – agent of human and societal destruction – assumed that a member of the Structural Gang Culture© would automatically succumb to the systemic racist agenda of the prison industrial complex. Le'Taxione® has proven you wrong and the world is privy to why and how one must "Change Gang Behavior from The Inside Out®".

Those who have been given positions of leadership within the struggle – who know they don't deserve them – and continue to drain the emotional, spiritual, and financial resources of the oppressed and marginalized – will recognize their reflection in Original Diamond Boy 2. You are documented in history and exposed to society once again. You have abandoned your word – oath – duties and have left the masses believing that you are an answered prayer. You are a detriment to yourself and your community – and have been concealing Le'Taxione® and his work from the youth and those who genuinely work towards social justice and change.

Then there is the issue of "justice". Society has accepted the unspoken price of justice and the suffering of those who cannot afford it. Le'Taxione® has not. Original Diamond Boy 2 will expose the reader to what it means to be a Diamond Boy while outnumbered in custody. This Diamond is beyond Hollywood depictions -political administrations – propaganda – miseducation – systemic campaigns to prevent someone from helping themselves -sabotage – blatant lies and court processes that commit more atrocities than those who are accused.

DIAMONDS ARE FOREVER. Created under pressure. You will overstand that Le'Taxione® is an author – Gangologist – educator – leader - legitimate business man – Concrete Activist – and a Structural Gang Culture© member who will not genuflect under the pressure of an unjust system and organizations with Nothing Accomplished After Considerable Pretense. HE IS A DIAMOND. He has work to do. He will not be deterred by individuals and formations content with theatrics and pretense. He will not be deterred by a system that continues to incarcerate him after they've admitted their own unjust practices. He is in perpetual motion. His work is his atonement.

Not only has he championed battles – he has recorded in various texts – including Gangology 101: Gang Violence Prevention and Intervention – the methodology that should be applied for another to fortify him or herself as they advance to mental and physical liberation. Be advised – however – that your leaders have kept this information from you. I've spoken to staff in Governor's offices. I've spent weeks in communications with members of the Black Caucus who claim to have an agenda on the behalf of the public. I can tell you – with respect the Gang Violence Prevention and Intervention – they are unprepared – untruthful – ill equipped – and interested in another bottom line.

THE TRUTH FEARS NO INVESTIGATION. This is something Le'Taxione® taught me very early. Check his work. Check his statements. You will know that he has been working on behalf of our communities for over thirty years – even during incarceration – without the assistance of the aforementioned. HE FEARS NO INVESTIGATION. However, our leaders and organizations of social justice and change cannot extend such an invitation – they're afraid you'll assess their progress and lack thereof.

The 2016 elections have consumed the public. Some may still have hope in the system. Some can't wait for the hype of politics to quiet down. Some are aware that the results mean noting to the Structural Gang Culture© and the communities blighted. Check the statistics of areas like Chicago and wonder why your President hasn't made the effort to help those of his hood – who look like him – to better their communities. Let that sink in.

The science of Le'Taxione®'s work facilitates positive change – from the inside out – accessible to all. Remember this when our leaders try to create groups of "us" and "they". These are age old social engineering strategies that maintain the societal divisions – oppression – and the prison industrial complex. Govern yourself accordingly. Find the truth – find the real – the inner resource – the path – and genuflect to no one. Stay the course. Le'Taxione® has done it and will continue to do so.

The oppression is real. The opposition is homicidal and genocidal

– the system is unjust – the leaders have sold out – the organizations have lost the moral compass required to stay the course – but –
DIAMONDS ARE FOREVER. Original Diamond Boy 2 will prove
just that.

Alafia Medina
Concrete Activist

Foreword

The documents that litter this book (interdepartmental emails, court documents, affidavits, etc.) were obtained through the Washington State Public Disclosure Act (RCW 42.56) and are authentic in their documentation of various attempts by it's prison administration and their insidious investigative units (I&I) in the Washington State Department of Corrections – to in my opinion – entrap, discredit my work, and or create a hostile environment that would in turn result in my assault.

The sophistry and subterfuge advanced by fifth columns that exist within prison administrations in the State of Washington is reprehensible, though not indicative of the character of all staff members in the penological system. For 20 years I've staved off attempts to discredit my work, and served numerous years in intensive management units (IMU) in the process because I stood on the truth and refused to capitulate in the face of adversity, contrary to the posture that most men made evident.

I refused to allow the penal system to use me as a saboteur – complicit in the dehumanization and degradation of men, in their attempt to procure recidivism, that they may garner job security and continue to supplement their income at the price of an incarcerated man's spirit.

I watched as men became spiritually destitute, morally bankrupt, and turned inside out – to reflect only a semblance of what The God created them to be. I visualized men becoming addicted to drugs, gambling, and become lovers of other men, never again to exhibit the characteristics of creativity or moral rectitude.

I witnessed men disrespect the feminine principle inherent in God Himself – by deceiving their mothers and their significant others only to pay off gambling and drug debts or for sexual trysts with other men. I've experienced the treachery and false representation of men – wherein the result gave rise to life or death circumstances; unbridled violence being the avenue most traveled in an attempt to exhibit manhood with all of the bravado that one could muster.

I watched the youth become haters of a woman's femininity and misogynistic in their interactions, seemingly more interested in and inordinate male bonding that closed the door on their natural developmental process, leaving them stagnate, holding any progress hostage, while investing in fantasy.

The realities are nurtured by injustice and inhumane treatment that only serves to endanger the public, as most of these men will eventually return to society. These facts in no way excuse the prisoner of his/her culpability or duty to take charge of his/her own reform in order to experience success upon their matriculation back into society – for inevitably – it is the prisoner's duty to secure his/her own success.

Le'Taxione®

Chapter One

"If prison is truly an industrial complex... and it is... And if every industry has to have a commodity... and it does... And since the prison industrial complex disproportionately houses Black men... One must reason that we are a commodity sanctioned by the 13th Amendment of the U.S. Constitution".

Le'Taxione®

While back in the general population at the Monroe Correctional Complex, I'd been made cognizant of the fact that a correctional officer, namely Sgt. Autry, had went to several incarcerated persons and made unflattering statements about me. In her attempt to garner disdain for me, she'd told numerous incarcerated persons that I was "a high-profile convict" and that "I was trouble". This was not the first time that correctional officers had made disparaging remarks about me. In their attempt to discredit my work, that attracted many incarcerated persons, and garnered the respect of all. Correctional officers would attempt to cast a cloud over my sincerity, while simultaneously casting accusations of surreptitious organizing of Afrikan Americans that could amount to a prison uprising.

Though this may seem unbelievable to taxpayers in so called

free society, the penological ideology, in its application behind these steel curtains, is oppressive and sinister to say the least. These insidious tactics, on behalf of correctional officers, are employed to discredit individuals that they feel have influence among incarcerated persons, which sometimes result in the assault of the person targeted by their slander.

I continued to maneuver and navigate the traps and snares set for me by the prison administration; continuing to work on my memoirs "Original Diamond Boy: Psychology of a Gangbanger" – which is now in the publishing stages. The relationship between Myisha and I suffered due to the elements of distance and time. The lack of human contact is a formidable opponent in any relationship – and the prison experience wasn't exempt. Now add a life sentence to the equation, which I was fighting, and any woman would become weary, disenchanted, and eventually discouraged.

"It's not normal for a man and woman who love each other, as we do, to be prohibited from engaging in the natural consummation of our love", Myisha would say.

"There's nothing normal or natural about this rotation. We knew this before we embarked upon this journey", I answered.

The fact is that once a man and woman make their intentions to become one known, an array of obstacles and enemies to their intentions make themselves evident. This fact is true in free society as well in the prison society. I've watched prison officials do everything in their power to discourage anyone who supports a prisoner in any capacity.

Chapter Two

I was transferred to the other side of the prison for reasons that at the time – were not readily available. I'd had issues with the custody unit supervisor (CUS) – which stemmed from a disagreement that we had when she was my counselor. I'd found out very early in my sentence that prison officials abhorred being corrected when they were operating outside of the policy – which not only governs incarcerated person's behavior – but also theirs.

Cognizant of this fact – I was stern with my correction of them when I found them in violation of the policy. I'd hold them accountable by filing complaints with the head of the Department of Corrections (DOC) – and though DOC would always rationalize its employees malfeasant behavior – the fact that a quasi-investigation was conducted brought attention to the rogue correctional officer and put him/her in a position to explain their unethical behavior.

This had been the case with CUS Howe, who had been my counselor. It was obvious that she had now used her position of authority to exercise reprisal against me – resulting in my arbitrary transfer to the other side of the prison. I didn't allow this fact to impede my progress. "As long as they don't stop the clock, I'm straight", I reasoned.

I'd begun taking college courses through the "University Behind

Bars". I enrolled in small business, sociology, and psychology. The instructor of my psychology class, Mrs. Barbara Bennett, PhD, was a very good instructor. She'd been very influential in my studies as she imparted knowledge in a manner that made it exciting to learn. When the bell rang for class – I'd be standing at the front of my assigned cell – books in hand – anxious to learn and express how I'd applied what I'd learned to the thought process of the Structural Gang Culture© experience.

My sociology instructor was an Afrikan American woman who was a great instructor also. What made her excellent was that she would take the principles of accepted sociology, apply them to accepted sociology – apply them to the Afrikan American experience and make it plausible.

I'd introduce to these instructors sociological and psychological concepts as the applied to the Structural Gang Culture© experience from them to critique and give me constructive criticism, which they did. In the course of our exchange – I decided to expand the N'STEP® curricula – incorporating the sociological aspects and elaborating on the psychological aspects of the Structural Gang Culture© experience. I began in earnest working on the second edition of the N'STEP® curriculum in early 2008.

Chapter Three

I t was in the best interest of self and community – that I obtained any aspect of education that was afforded to me – but it had to be real education. A wise man once said that "Education is a process that allows one to more effectively be himself". Considering the fact that the word education comes from the Latin E-duco – meaning to lead out of or away from ignorance. I found the above said saying not only true – but imperative.

I'd watch as some – in the Afrikan American community – obtain what they perceived to be an education – only to join peripheral organizations – or a job market whose interest behind the veil – was detrimental to our communities. This made evident the fact that they were not truly educated… they were trained. Trained to perpetuate the status quo – which was diametrically opposed to justice and equality; hence detrimental to the interest of the huddled masses. Now some may question my right to speak as I do – citing that all my life I'd been one of the major contributors to the genocide that plagued our communities – but as the scripture says, "When I was a child I spake as a child, but when I became a man I put away childish things".

There comes a time in one's life when he must refuse to be an element produced by environment; and begin to produce circumstances that change one's environment – and one can only accomplish this through reeducation – which fuels the light of desire and in turn feeds the will. This is what takes dreams out of the realm of phantasmagorical intangibility and places them in the realm of possibility.

A dream that is not acted upon after it is experienced – is just that… a dream. But when one has a dream and his/her next waking moment is spent attempting to make that dream a reality, that is no longer a dream… it is a vision. I had a vision that could effectuate change in impoverished communities across America – and therein lies my work – and I couldn't let that fact that I was physically apprehended – result in the stagnation that kept one psychologically captured.

Chapter Four

One day after an intense workout in the weight room, I sat in my assigned cell waiting to be allowed to take a shower – when my comrade Oak from Compton walked up and told me that my brother, Soldier Boy, was in the infirmary getting medical attention – and that he'd sent him to come get me so that we could talk. The first emotion to wash over me was anger. Soldier Boy had been released from prison in 1999 and I'd not heard from him while he was on the bricks, though I'd always hear from him when he'd fall (get incarcerated) and have to serve a little time.

"How dare he think that he could send for me at the drop of a hat and I'd come running to see him", I thought.

Anger was quickly replaced by longing and I began to get dressed so that I may catch a glimpse of my brother and maybe share a stolen moment. After all, I loved my brother and longed for a familiar face, one that truly knew me and loved me unconditionally. I anxiously walked down the long prison corridor without regard for any rules or regulations. I knew that if I was caught in movement that I could be cuffed up and taken to the SHU (segregation) – but that was a small price to pay to see my brother.

As I entered the infirmary, I saw Soldier standing in a cage waiting to be seen. He was noticeably thin, his face grey from a lack of electrolytes and he was missing a tooth. Internally I cringed at the sight of him. This was not my brother. This was a shell of what he used to be.

I flashed a smile and said, "West up Soldier?"

"West up, Cuzzin?" Soldier yelled in excitement.

"How you doin' Homie, you alright?" Soldier asked.

I could see that he'd fallen victim and had become dependent on synthetic chemicals. The ingestion of these chemicals had caused him to fall down on all fours psychologically and subvert street piety© in pursuit of escape. He was dead mentally and spiritually – yet he genuinely asked about my well-being.

"Don't worry about me Soldier! I'm good. I've not allowed this time to kill my spirit. I stay in perpetual motion" I answered.

"What did you come with (How much time did you get?" I asked.

"I just got a violation. I'll be out in 30 days" he answered.

I told Soldier that I loved him with all that is me and to take care of himself, then I spinned and walked off. I almost cried on my way back to my assigned cell. It took all I could muster to not break down in front of Soldier. It killed me inside to see him in that condition – under that circumstance. Though I saw death on him spiritually, his eyes sparkled at the sight of me – his big brother.

I said a silent prayer while in movement – "God please protect my brother and give me liberation from my present circumstance , so that I may intervene in his self-destruction and guide him to a more sustainable circumstance".

Chapter Five

Finally, "Original Diamond Boy: Psychology of a Gangbanger" was published and I had it in my hands. This was my second publication and I couldn't wait to show it to my comrades behind the steel curtains.

Mrs. Barbara Bennett, PhD., had graciously written the content on the back page of my book and I longed to show it to her. After evaluating why it was so important for me to present my book to Mrs. Bennett, I found that "I sought her approval". I respected her intellect, her humanness, and her opinion. I saw her in a light that she would probably not be able to countenance – for I saw her divinely.

I'd suffered so much injustice at the hands of Caucasians in my life experiences that I'd become apprehensive and distrustful of them, but there had been two Caucasians that had now been placed in my path; Mrs. Bennett, PhD., and Mr. Jeff Ellis, my attorney, and I felt that God was showing me wisdom through both of these integrity driven, justice-seeking people.

Mrs. Bennett's eyes lit up when she saw my book. I could tell that she was genuinely happy for me and at the same time proud of me. This fact motivated and inspired me to keep diagnosing elements of the Structural Gang Culture© mentality and prescribing the panacea for the trauma that perpetuated it – and I did.

I'd hired attorney Jeff Ellis to represent me in my criminal appeal. It would prove to be an uphill battle for the negligence and unethical practice exhibited by my previous appeal attorney. Those practices resulted in a dismissal of my habeas petition – with prejudice – meaning that I could no longer petition the court for my liberation – Game Over! We refused to accept that. Jeff Ellis was an attorney with moral rectitude. He loved justice and fought on the side of justice.

He didn't have that "public pretender" mentality that was prevalent amongst the legal community who were appointed to represent defendants by the courts. He was a man of integrity, professionalism, ethics, and honor. Upon accepting my case, he expressed the mediocrity of the representation that I'd received and assured me that he would not only represent me vigorously, but that he would fight as long as it took to secure me liberation.

Mr. Ellis went directly to work filing a Personal Restraint Petition (PRP) on my behalf – arguing – among other things – that my California class C felony should have not been used in the calculation of my three strikes sentence – that the Washington State Supreme Court applied a non-Constitutional standard concerning me being shackled during the trial – wherein the jury was able to view the shackles – then placing the burden on me to prove that the fact that the jury saw me in shackles during trial prejudiced me – which in all reality it is the prosecutor's burden to prove that the shackles didn't prejudice me.

For these facts – I was given a sentence that exceeded the court's jurisdiction – for I was not a persistent offender (three striker). Then he argued that justice demanded that my conviction be vacated and that I be re-sentenced. Now the waiting game began. We had several hurdles to overcome in my case. The first one was to prove to the Appellate

Courts that my case had merit and should be allowed to proceed on said merits. This would be hard, for the ineffectiveness of my previous appeal attorneys had rendered me time barred – meaning that I'd run out of time to fight for my liberation.

Ponder that concept. Because one has not continued to litigate his/her case within a 1 year time frame – one loses the right to ever demand his/her liberation unless a new law or a "material change in the law" directly affects his/her case. So, if one does not know the law and is misrepresented by appointed counsel – one can lose his/her right to litigate for his/her liberation.

How can one place a time frame on justice?! What is more un-just than telling a man that he's waited too long to present issues in a judicial manner? One year is not enough time to learn the law in order to present an appeal for justice, and on top of that, the law that you must learn derives from Latin terms.

Most of us in the Hood don't have a firm grasp on English and we've been in America all our lives. Now that we've been convicted of a crime – we must learn law – in a Latin language – within one year – lest we lose our right to litigate for our liberation. And this is called justice?!

And what should we make of a judicial system wherein one who is accused of a crime cannot represent himself effectively in court, for he does not know the proper terminology? Any judicial system wherein truth is not enough to gain one's liberation, and one must be held to the standard of an attorney who's studied years to learn his/her craft – is not a judicial system. For a "judicial system", in its ap-plication, denotes the administration of justice. On the contrary, what we face as laymen to the law, is a secret society – masquerading as a judicial system – which can only be accessed through secret codes, terminologies, and gestures. Yet, we are depicted as the criminal.

Chapter Six

Though I'd extended the opportunity to some of the brothers that I rotated with on a continuum to contribute to the N'STEP® Second Edition Gangology 101© - there was only one brother who accepted the offer and worked earnestly to contribute. This was a brother name Dawud. Dawud was a very loyal brother who was without the cancer of envy, and in that spirit, he provided me with the research I requested of him – earning himself the title of Research Assistant. This brother had been a part of the Structural Gang Culture© and he honestly wanted to see me succeed.

In May of 2008, unbeknownst to us, the Hilltop and Lakewood Crips had disciplined two of their homeboys for violating their dictates. This discipline resulted in the assault of two of their members, and though I'm from California, I would find out later that it was said that I'd ordered the assault of these Crips, for their disrespect of the code.

As Dawud and myself were sitting in the prison's activity room working on Gangology 101©, on of the brothers that were disciplined by the Hilltop and Lakewood Crips approached my table and informed me that while he was in the SHU, two officers of the Intelligence and Investigations Unit (I&I) had told him that I had, in fact, ordered his assault. I immediately rose from my seat, taking on an aggressive posture and stated, "What's the demonstration?!"

If the brother had even moved wrong I would have moved against him relentlessly, but the brother stated, "I told them that I didn't believe that because I knew you and that you were not on that page."

I searched the brother's face for animosity – there was none.

"Are you willing to write me and affidavit stating what I&I had told you about me?"

"Yes", he answered.

Coming in from the yard were approximately thirteen people. Crips, Gangster Disciples, and Skinheads. There was a racial riot. They were handcuffed and then taken to the SHU. The whole prison went on lockdown. I pondered the significance of what had happened and though I was not a part of the initial riot – the fact that it was a racial riot had far-reaching implications. I didn't need this, but it if involved blacks – it involved me. There was no such thing, in prison politics, that discriminated between which Blacks or Whites were in the riot. Prison politics dictated that once it was ignited – everyone was a potential target.

Word came from the SHU that it was the Skinheads that initiated the confrontation and that the brothers obliged them by aggressively silencing the struggle. I smiled out loud.

Chapter Seven

On July 3, 2008 – while preparing to go to the gym – seven officers suddenly appeared in front of my assigned cell – cuffed me and transported me to the SHU. As always, none of the transporting officers knew why I was being placed in the SHU. When asked, they articulated the status quo position "We don't know. They'll serve you with papers when you are received."

I arrived at the SHU and was taken through the dehumanizing and intrusive process called a strip search – which entailed me getting naked, bending over and coughing while several correctional officers watched. This is one of the most degrading things that a man could experience and it is my perception that it is done for this reason. It reminded me of slaves on the auction block and the correctional officers that watched acted with the same disdain and malice that slave masters acted with during the slave experience.

I was then given an orange jumpsuit, cuffed, and escorted to my assigned cell in the SHU. As I walked down the tier, I could hear the everyday madness that was concomitant with this form of lockdown. The yelling, the banging, the screaming, the pain, the oppression, the injustice. All of these things were audible in my walk down the tier – but I had been here before – and as a coping mechanism – I returned there mentally in that instance.

Once I got into my assigned cell, someone yelled, "Who dat is?!"

"Le'Taxione!" I replied.

Then I asked, "Who is that?"

"It's Choke" the voice returned.

Choke was one of my young comrades that I'd done time with at Washington State Penitentiary. He'd gotten released and in the time frame of a couple of years he'd returned for a murder. He happened to be one of the Crips involved in the race riot.

"Sajadalahu Comrade!" I shot back at him.

"What did they arrest you for?" Choke asked.

Behind these steel curtains there was too – a free society (general population) and an incarcerated society (the SHU). When one was taken to the SHU, we spoke of him being arrested.

"I don't know Comrade, but they'll be serving me my paperwork in a minute!" I replied.

No sooner than I made that statement an officer came to my assigned cell door with my paperwork.

"I'm here to issue you your segregation authorization forms", He stated with a sinister grin.

After reading the forms I found that I had been placed in the SHU for reasons that amounted to me ordering the assault of the two Crips in the weight room and orchestrating the assault on the Skinheads by the Crips and the Gangster Disciples.

"Choke!" I yelled.

"Yeah!" He answered.

"They got me for orchestrating assaults and the little riot they got you for."

"Peep game Comrade. I got to get at you about that when there's not so many ears on the tier" Choke said.

"Go to the yard tomorrow and shoot me a script" I replied.

Even while in the SHU, we were allowed to have a court mandated 1 hour of recreation a day and three showers a week. My plan was for Choke to go to the yard – which consisted of four cement walls, a phone, pull-up and dip bars – and leave me a note that I would retrieve when I went to the yard.

"That won't work Comrade. The cameras out there have been updated and they'll intercept that. I'll hit the showers in the morning and touch your hand" Choke said.

Choke's plan was to write the script, warp it in plastic taken from our food tray, and leave it in the shower for me to retrieve when it was my turn to take my shower.

"Ndio, Kiwe" (Yes, Cousin), I answered him in Swahili to remind him that this is the way we will communicate this particular incident.

"Mimi upendo wewe Kiwe" (I love you cousin), Choke replied.

"Mpaka kifo tufanye Kiwe" (Until death do us Cousin), I said – and then started my SHU workout.

Chapter Eight

The next morning, I woke up at 4:30 a.m. as usual. After praying, I began reading my Bible. Once again, I found myself in the Gospels. I always found comfort in the trials and tribulations that Jesus was faced with. I did not see Scripture in only the historical sense. I reasoned that those who did not get the electrical inner meanings of the Word of God that were made manifest in His chosen servants. I see Scripture as 25% manifested in the time it was being experienced in and 75% revealed as it applied to future tense.

This being my personal truth, when I read the Gospels, I applied them to my present circumstance – which in turn gave me the extra needed strength to navigate the sophistry, subterfuge. And evil machinations that were being superimposed upon me by not only the prison administration, but also those who constituted the prison population that were stagnate in their application of truth and progressive thought.

After my studies, I prayed again and got ready to go to the yard to use the phone. Once escorted to the yard and the chains were removed from my hands through a cuff port, I called Myisha. After hearing that I was in the SHU, I could hear in her voice that she was distraught.

"They're going to keep violating my civil rights until I sue them.

The only thing that they respect is litigation" I said.

Myisha didn't understand the dynamics that surrounded me in this toxic environment called prison – and because of this fact – we'd, for the most part, be in disagreement as to the strategy that would be most efficacious to secure justice in this particular instance. We came from two different regions, with two separate experiences, which procured two different lifestyles and psychologies that informed how we dealt with circumstances and events.

Though I didn't want to entertain the though, I knew that this trial would prove to be intense, creating an oppositional force that would cause her to detach in order to protect herself emotionally – and that said detachment – in turn – would cause me to erect walls, wherein I could protect my heart in preparation of her imminent abandonment.

This was a tried, tested, and proven effective tactic used by the Department of Corrections – motivated by racism, while in the same breath feigning their desire for the incarcerated person to maintain and sustain his/her community support.

Though Myisha followed the instructions given to perpetuate my strategy, I could tell that she'd grown weary of this struggle – and that fact garnered – in my opinion – half-hearted attempts at exacting justice… in this instance. The fact is, she didn't sign up for this. It wasn't her intentions to engage the prison administration in psychological warfare. All she wanted to do was support the work of a man who wanted to ameliorate the conditions in our communities.

She could not fathom why one who'd reformed, transformed, and given his life to Changing Gang Behavior From the Inside Out© could be on the receiving end of hostility from those who put policies and programs in place to effect the reformation of the incarcerated person. She became jaded in the injustice I was subjected to and I watched the light of desire in her dissipate, though she was unaware.

Chapter Nine

I expressed my sincere affections for Myisha then hung up the phone. I didn't like to see weakness I those that I revered, and I heard what I thought was weakness in her, and that disgusted me.

Two correctional officers appeared at the yard door and requested me to turn around backwards and put my hands through the cuff port in order to be handcuffed and escorted me to the shower. The shower in and of itself was an entirely different experience. It consisted of what was no more than a cell with a nozzle, plexi-glass covering the bar and a tin mirror in which you could not see your reflection.

Once the correctional officers uncuffed me and left the tier, I hollered at the comrade Choke.

"Kiwe!", I yelled.

"Ndio", he answered.

"Wapi ile karatasi?" (Where's the paper?), I asked.

Choke said one word, "sabuni" (soap).

I looked on the floor and their lied a piece of hollowed out soap. I picked up, retrieved the note that was wrapped in plastic and yelled "Asante sana!" (Thank you).

"Kukuaa nguvu Askari" (Stay strong soldier), Choke said.

"Sio shaka" (No doubt), I replied.

I finished showering and was escorted back to my assigned cell. Once the correctional officers left, I read the script.

"Say, Cuzz, when I&I questioned me about the demonstration, the one named Frantz tried to get me to implicate you. He even implied that if I was to tell him it was orchestrated by you that my sanction would be lighter. I told him that Le'Taxione is so far removed from this kind of thing that it was not only laughable that they were trying to implicate you, but it was the same racist mindset that caused the problem. Comrade, I've been at two separate facilities with you and watched you conduct yourself impeccably – but these administrations continue to oppress you and your progress. Why do you even try?"

Your Comrade,
Choke

After I read the script, I sat back and pondered Choke's concerns. He was 100% correct. He'd been at the Washington State Penitentiary with me and witnessed the same racist and oppressive tactics used there – against me. The mind of a racist is so insidious, and in most instances inherent, that for the most part – he/she doesn't even realize that his/her behavior is in fact racist. They've grown up in a society that perpetuates white privilege, meaning the color of their skin affords them opportunities that are not afforded to the people of color.

The fact is validated by exhaustive studies and data – but this was only one insidious form of racism. The other form is surreptitious. This form of racism is consciously practiced and said practice is exacerbated by authority. That was what I was experiencing in the Washington State Department of Corrections (WDOC). Rampant, vitriol racism that went unchecked by the upper echelon in the department – and this is what allowed it to not only exist – but to thrive at an infectious rate.

Though there were correctional officers that were not racist, they would turn a blind eye to the blatant racism of their colleagues which made them complicit in the mistreatment of the Afrikan American population. Messages continued to come to me through the grapevine from Crips, Gangster Disciples, and even the Skinheads, stating that I&I unit officers Frantz and Hoosier were attempting to coerce those that were involved in the assault and subsequent riot to implicate me, and even offered lighter sanctions if they'd do so.

Of course, none involved implicated me. That was not due to a prison code. On the contrary, the prison code in this state had long become nonexistent. No one implicated me because I had nothing to do with either incident. At that moment I realized the tactic that I&I was advancing. First, they would attempt to coerce those who were actually involved in the assault and subsequent riot to implicate me – and when coercion failed, they would prevaricatively tell them that I orchestrated the assaults. This was a sanctioned attempt by the administration to have me green lighted (assaulted) by these different groups.

This transpires all the time behind these steel curtains, unbeknownst to those taxpayers that by silence, give the Department of Corrections great latitude in dealing with America's prison population in general – and the state of Washington's prison population in particular. At that moment I decided I would need to file a 1983 Civil Complaint against the officers at the Monroe Complex.

Chapter Ten

I began ordering case law from the legal library to research how to file a civil complaint and the recent law concerning my present position and circumstance. In doing so, I found that civil complaints of this nature were commonplace. I took that to mean that the racist mentality – exacerbated by authority – was prevalent throughout America's prisons and that Afrikan Americans were disproportionately on the receiving end of this racism.

This being the fact, I contacted prisoners' rights groups such as Columbia Legal Services and the ACLU – both of Washington. After contacting several private attorneys, it became painfully evident that no one was willing to sue the Department of Corrections. I even contacted, through a complaint, the U.S. Department of Justice, but no one would even investigate my grievance… I found that various prisoner's rights groups were contracted by either the Department of Corrections or those directly affiliated with the DOC.

This seemed to me, to be more than a conflict of interest. It was an all-out affront on the integrity of legal services that they were supposed to render to prisoners.

"How could they be a fair representative of prisoners when both were either paid by the DOC or had their checks issued from the same source?" I reasoned.

Though the Department of Corrections would have their legal representative, the Attorney General, and an abundance of resources and personnel at their disposal – this fact didn't intimidate me in the least. My life had been placed in danger and my only redress would be through the courts. This meant that I would have to challenge the Goliath by myself – so I continued to prepare.

Chapter Eleven

I'd extended through Myisha, my willingness to not only take a polygraph exam to prove that I had no involvement with the recent violence at that facility, but I also expressed my willingness to pay for said polygraph test. I'd witnessed the I&I Unit conduct polygraphs on incarcerated persons that were suspected of selling drugs or compromising staff and both Myisha and myself though that if they truly sought the truth of the matter, they would entertain my request.

This was the only way that I could prove that I was innocent of these horrid allegations – but even though we'd submitted this request to not only the I&I Unit and the warden of the prison – but also the head of the Washington State Department of Corrections in Olympia, Washington – the request was denied.

This was made pellucid the fact that there was no desire on behalf of the prison administration of the Department of Corrections to ferret out the truth, and soon after, though I was not given an infraction, nor found guilty of any misconduct – I was arbitrarily and capriciously transferred out to the Clallam Bay Corrections Center. One of the most racist and oppressive prison facilities in the state of Washington.

A transfer that even the Head of the Department of Corrections denied any knowledge of.

Chapter Twelve

The Clallam Bay Corrections Center (CBCC) was located near Canada. It was said that it existed in a rainforest and because it rained constantly without cessation – I believed it. When I arrived at CBCC, I immediately took notice of the blatantly racist climate and knew that this climate would test the very fabric of me.

After being processed and sent to D-Unit, where all the arrivals from different facilities were housed before being placed in the general population, I was told that I had an interview. I didn't ask who'd requested the interview because I knew the answer would be the status quo reply – and considering the overtly racist climate – I thought it best to wait until I was in the presence of those who'd requested to interview me to present any questions.

I was escorted to a small room that looked like a conference room where two women sat.

"My name is Mrs. Swunsen. I'm the Associate Superintendent and this is Mrs. Talmer. She's and I&I unit officer", Mrs. Swunsen said.

"Hello, Le'Taxione", Mrs. Talmer said.

"Hello" I replied, then sat down.

It was clear that it was Mrs. Swunsen that had requested the interview – for she did all of the talking while Mrs. Talmer acted in the capacity of witness and support for the Associate Superintendent.

"I was asked by the Director of Prisons to speak with you concerning your transfer here and to assure you that they would be investigating your complaints concerning I&I unit officers Frantz, Hoover, and Tarnish", Mrs. Swunsen stated.

I didn't go into detail about the posture that I'd taken concerning the issue – because to do so would be a tactic, and tactics are the results of incomplete thoughts. I was a strategist and strategizing required exhaustive thought.

"I can see the difference in climate at this facility – and in my very short time here I've already witnessed the discriminatory manner in which Afrikan Americans are treated as opposed to the Caucasian counterparts", I stated.

I wanted the Associate Superintendent to know that the tactics that were employed by correctional officers under her supervision, were in the least, discriminative, and that I would speak out against these injustices – regardless of the consequences.

"I want to assure you Le'Taxione, that I don't tolerate discrimination or racism of any kind and neither does Mrs. Talmer. If you see these behaviors in any of my staff, I want to know about it", Mrs. Swunsen said.

"I'm sure you've been briefed before my arrival. I sincerely hope that you don't have any preconceived notions about me that would cause you or your subordinates to treat me in a discriminative manner", I stated.

"We have discussed your institutional record, and as you are aware, you are considered a high-profile inmate – but I guarantee that you will be treated within institutional policy", Mrs. Swunsen answered.

"Also, I am a published author and gangologist. I hope that my work will not garner me the Security Threat Group (STG) title and result in me being placed in the SHU", I stated.

For the first time, Mrs. Talmer spoke. "I am the senior officer of the I&I unit and I am aware of your work. If you have any problems concerning your work, have the correctional officers contact me. In the meantime, while you are writing books, place your writing tablet in a manilla envelope with the title of book on it when you are not in your cell, so that if your cell is searched, correctional officers will not think that your books are STG material".

I affirmed that I would be in compliance with Mrs. Talmer's suggestion and was escorted back to my assigned cell. Once I got there, I replayed everything about that interview from the texture to the tone of their voices, body language, and what was not said...Then I smiled out loud.

Chapter Thirteen

Visually I'd taken stock of the ethnic disparities in the prison population at CBCC. This was a facility that was predominately Caucasian and historically a haven for white supremacist Skinheads. I'd done approximately two years in this facilities SHU back in 2002, at which time the Skinheads had stabbed a couple Afrikan Americans. I began to ponder the fact that while in transit I was told by a Skinhead that I&I unit officer Frantz had told him that I'd orchestrated the assault on the Skinheads at Monroe Correctional Complex (MCC/WSR). I knew what I had to do.

As soon as I was allowed to hit the yard, I would confront the Skinhead representative. I couldn't walk around this facility not knowing if they'd planned on greenlighting me. If they had an issue with the information that had been artfully disseminated by Frantz, we'd handle it right then. The announcement for yard blared over the intercom, "Yard for D-unit! Yard for D-Unit!"

I emerged from the unit and walked swiftly down the breezeway into the yard. It was imperative that I got to the yard before it became saturated with people. I needed to be able to visualize the mannerisms and activity of the Skinheads as they congregated. While observing, my Damu comrade from Cali named P approached me.

"What's up, Le'Taxione?" he greeted me.

"Same grind, different time", I replied without looking at him.

"What's going down?", P asked.

"I got to get at these Skinheads in case they got beef", I replied.

"Let's get at um", P said.

As we approached them, I could see the inquisitive looks on their faces. This informed me that they were not aware of a pending issue. As we invaded their circle I spoke.

"My name is Le'Taxione and I was transferred here for the riot at Monroe."

It was so quiet you could hear a mouse pissing on cotton.

"Is there any problems we have to handle?" I asked.

"We don't have any problems with you Le'Taxione", one of the Skinheads that had done time with me at Walla Walla said.

When P and I turned to walk away, we noticed that other Afrikan Americans on the yard had taken notice of our demonstration and had come together in a group. The Skinheads had also noticed this and because this was not a normal occurrence, it probably looked to them that the move was organized, but it wasn't. I played on the Skinhead's perception by directly walking up to the group, who in turn showered me with greeting and introduction.

For that moment in time, I was the recipient of Black love – but I knew through experience that this would be short lived – at least on this grand scale. My demonstration, political views, ideology, abrasive character, and refusal to bite my tongue on any issue made me a polarizing figure, and the fact that I was from California on exacerbated this fact.

It seemed that those from Washington – for the most part – fostered a love/hate relationship with those of use from Cali. On one hand, they loved out demonstration, but on the other hand it seemed as though they hated the fact that they were reduced to merely mimicking the lifestyle of those from California. This critique isn't meant to paint the whole with such a broad brush, for it is the fact that I've been blessed to be in the company of some very intelligent, honorable cats from Washington – and I respect them to the fullest – but they are few and far between.

I returned to my assigned cell and reflected on what had just transpired. Once they'd opened the dayroom, I was afforded the opportunity to use the phone. On my way, I was approached by one of the Skinheads.

"Aye, Le'Taxione. Can I talk to you?" he asked.

I immediately scanned his face, his body language, his stance, and then his torso for any bulges – all in one full swoop of my glance. This quick inspection would let me know his mood, his motives, his intentions, if said intentions were to my detriment, and did he have a weapon to procure his desired result.

Though he obviously had no weapon, I remained hypervigilant and said, "What's going down?"

He walked to a secluded area and I followed. Once we were where he felt comfortable, out of earshot of other inmates, he stated, "Look, our brother Fillion sent word to that the I&I unit officer Frantz told him during an interview that you authorized the greenlight on our brothers at Monroe, but he also said he didn't believe that it was true. Fillion is a solid White Boy and we take his word over a piece of shit cop any day".

It was obvious that this cat was sent to inform me of the Skinhead's position on this issue.

"I respect your stance", I said.

"We don't have any problems with you Le'Taxione – but this is our yard", he stated.

"That may be true, but I'm going to demonstrate how I want to demonstrate", I replied.

He was taking a passive/aggressive stance. Though they didn't want problems, they didn't want to be viewed as cowards, hence his statement "This is our yard". So, I too, advanced in the same manner by letting him know that I am cognizant of the fact that the skinheads are the disproportionate majority at this facility, but that fact would not be seem by me as a restriction on my movement. In doing so, I gave him a backdoor wherein he could report to their shot caller that he'd delivered the message in its totality. I spun and went to the phone.

Chapter Fourteen

I got through to Myisha and let her know that I had touched down and that after engaging the opposition, things seemed cool. She sighed in relief. We'd been at opposite ends concerning how to address the fact that the I&I unit at Monroe attempted to have me greenlighted. First by the Crips and then the Skinheads. Myisha wanted to take the path of least resistance – for she thought that to agitate aggressively would only cause correctional officers to target me more intensely. She failed to realize, I her experience, that if I didn't agitate aggressively it would surely cause me to continue to be targeted – which would surely result me in being greenlighted by one of the many Security Threat Groups behind these steel curtains.

I decided to file a 1983 Civil Complaint against the staff at Monroe which would detail their discrimination, racism, and attempt to procure my assault by fabricating intelligence and disseminating it among the Security Threat Group population. I began gathering documentation to prove my case and was astonished at what my investigation unearthed. As said documents were made available and/or allotted to me by various means, the targeting began in earnest.

The correctional officers at CBCC, though not as bright as the I&I unit at Monroe, was just as racist and insidious as the machinations. They began to use the cell search procedure as a tool to discourage my efforts to build a case against their "fellow officers". They began stealing legal documents from the legal boxes in my assigned cell and I began filing complaints against them.

I found out early in civil litigation that to preserve my issues in court, I had to exhaust my remedies on the administrative level, lest the charges that I'd leveled against this "Fifth Column" that existed within the prison administration's in the Washington State Department of Corrections, would be dismissed.

So, I preserved my issues through complaints, continued procuring the documentation needed to support my claims and stood firm in the face of racism – masked by authority in the form of prison correctional officers.

Chapter Fifteen

In August of 2008 I was called to the officer's station and issued legal mail. When I saw that it was from my attorney, Jeff Ellis, I was both apprehensive and anxious about the possibilities. It could have been bad news notifying me that my Personal Restraint Petition (PRP) was without and my attempt to secure my liberation had failed – or it could have been good news notifying me that my PRP was in fact meritorious and that it would be scheduled for oral arguments in front of a three judge panel – who would then determine if I could proceed through the courts in my attempts to secure my liberation. It was the latter... My case was scheduled for oral arguments in December of 2008.

In the months preceding my December court date, I was made painfully aware that Myisha and I, plagued by distance and time, were growing apart. For some, the sullen grey walls of the prison industrial complex are insurmountable. This being the case, they allow the superficial barriers impede personal and intimate human contact to become larger than life, marring their path to happiness to the point that they emotionally abandon the object of their affection – whether consciously or subconsciously.

I'd informed Myisha that my transfer to this prison was intended to procure isolation and eradicate my support system – at which time she said – with all the confidence she could muster, "Nothing that DOC could do could cause her to abandon me", yet this was exactly what was taking place.

I'd call her less often in order to save money. In my mind, this arbitrary transfer to this region was the beginning of the end and I watched it as if it was one of those painfully tragic love stories, wherein the love that was professed between the main characters was based upon proximity, rather then authenticity. Some people say that "absence makes the heart grow fonder". I say that "absence makes the heart go yonder", and I was bearing witness to this fact in my own personal relationship.

That being expressed, I had not the time to properly bury any emotions that I still entertained for Myisha – so I redirected my focus to securing my liberation and protecting myself through civil litigation.

Chapter Sixteen

I was transferred to Ccccc-Unit and placed in an assigned cell with a cat named Evil from Los Angeles's Village Town Piru. Because my Structural Gang Culture© was Diamond Crips, I saw this as yet another attempt to put me into an uncomfortable and possibly dangerous position.

Evil was a light-skinned brother who stood about 5'7", 260 lbs., and muscular. To someone who'd not lived the life that I'd lived, Evil would have been very intimidating, but I was from the streets, and I'd engaged the enemy of this stature on a continuum, and I wasn't a little guy myself.

I prepared myself for confrontation. The fact that we were both from The Land (California) allowed us to see past the Colors that we represented in the expression of our separate experiences and realities. At first, Evil didn't like the fact that they'd moved me into his assigned cell. As we begam to dialogue, we found that we had more in common than we thought.

He conveyed his reality to me and I to him. In the midst of this discourse, I found that he'd been sentenced for murder and that the informant in his case had done time at WSP with me. When he conveyed who the informant was, there was no stretch of imagination needed to see the boy in that light. His character while at WSP was suspect, to say the least. He'd never been one of integrity and even his attempt to portray himself as a Crip was half-hearted.

After hearing the totality of the logistics wrapped around Evil's alleged crime, I was disheartened. My heart cried for him, for I knew what he would be faced with while doing time in this particular region. Although, I didn't reveal my experiences during times when we'd converse. My love for the land and those trapped this far away from familiarity and the intensity of the experience never subsided.

Evil and I became fast comrades. He was someone that understood and represented a Code of Ethics marked by loyalty, honor, respect, and integrity. We'd come from the Cali reality and that governed our interactions. We both held on dearly to what Cali had taught us in the streets. We fostered and nurtured the principles that cultivated and shaped us. As I would sit back and ponder these facts in the recesses of my mind, my heart would scream out loud, "I love this Cali shit!"

Chapter Seventeen

I began writing my first urban fiction entitled "Street Poisoned". Evil worked in the institution kitchen. His work hours were from 4:00 a.m. to 11:00 a.m. - so I did most of my writing while he was at work. Instead of the envy that I'd experienced with the vast majority of those who were ironically the object of my struggle in the system. Evil wholeheartedly supported my work without reservations. I'd be so excited about the progress that I was making on the book that I'd read from it's chapters when Evil returned to our assigned cell from work to get his reaction – and not once did he exhibit a lack of interest in my work. In fact, he'd grown to expect and even look forward to hearing chapters from the book and delighted in my dramatic recitals.

I'd see that genuine interest and appreciation in his eyes when I'd read to him. It was like my words took him home to a familiar place, allowing him to relive familiar events and circumstances that he'd secretly longed for. Those events and circumstances, though violent, represented normalcy for those of us subjected to the trauma of constant poverty, environmental violence, and the Structural Gang Culture© conformist ideology©

Chapter Eighteen

Yes, we were psychologically wounded. We'd experienced some of the most horrific acts of violence and loss of life imaginable right there in our communities. Our environment demanded violence of us, and not to oblige designated us as victims, so we became violent and aggressive in our environment. We superimposed our will through fear. No one else knew that that imposition rose out of fear. This fear was not the obvious fear of death. Hell, we embraced the reality of death and some subconsciously longed for it, but our fear was more insidious and systemic. We feared poverty, we feared victimization, we feared irrelevance!

I continued to endure retaliation in the form of cell searches, and I continued investigating the rogue staff at CBCC through the vehicle of Public Disclosure. I found, among other things, that the tactic of retaliatory cell searches, which resulted in the veiled confiscation of legal documents, was the norm at this facility.

Not only was the retaliatory cell searches and veiled confiscation of legal documents the norm, but the placing of razors in cells was also a well-documented tactic used by prison staff at CBCC when they were targeting those whose political ideology was deemed contradictory to their penological objective, which was to sustain job security through recidivism.

I was used to these tactics and continued to preserve these issues for imminent litigation through the grievance process which was in and of itself tainted. The Grievance Coordinated was a little obese woman who rode to work on the same bus as some of the staff, making it impossible to be an impartial fact finder in the process of redress. She would often times send the most damaging complaints back to me, for one reason or another, in an attempt to discourage me, in hopes that I would abandon the process. However, I was cognizant of the fact that if I had not followed the process, as prescribed, I would lose my right to bring my complaint before the courts – so I remained impervious in my pursuit to exhaust my remedies.

When she realized that returning my complaints to me for frivolous reasons would not deter me, she began filing my complaints inappropriately. Those complaints that alleged serious violations of my civil rights were supposed to be filed as staff misconduct complaints. Filed in this manner, they would garner serious corrective measures. Armed with this knowledge and colored by the interpersonal relationships that she entertained with staff, she would not process my complaints in the proper manner, violating the very policy that governed the grievance complaint process, undermining its integrity.

There were two specific correctional officers that worked D-Unit where I was housed, that were the personification of rogue staff. C/O Cram and C/O Defuss. These specific C/O's were well known for using the cell search process as a tool for retaliation. The fact that these officers were rogue was well documented by complaints against them that resulted them in being investigated and though investigations were conducted, the atmosphere of racist nepotism was so incestuous that said investigations would only result in letters of remand – as in the case of C/O Cram who was reprimanded for spitting in inmate's food while working in the kitchen.

The "Union", which protects the interest of the correctional officers at CBCC, was very strong I their representation. So strong that that criminal behaviors of the officers were vigorously defended in behind closed-door sessions with the administration. The interchangeable relationship was evil and symbiotic, attacking anyone who dared to advance in an attempt to procure accountability for the officer's criminal behavior. This fact alone was enough to discourage the grievant. The retaliatory cell searches continued, the confiscation of my legal documents, which were exhibits in my case against the Department of Corrections staff, continued, as did the filing of complaints on my part, without reticence.

Chapter Nineteen

In September 2008, Mr. Ellis notified me via legal mail, that we were granted oral arguments in front of a three-judge panel in early December 2008. I was excited! This was the beginning of the end of my unjust incarceration.

Myisha was too, excited and promised to attend my oral arguments. Though our relationship in my mind, had begun to show signs of withering, it was obvious that she still wanted what was best for me. She prayed fervently for my liberation and I found solace in that fact. She was always there for me, in her support, though I saw signs of us becoming more distant emotionally.

I didn't think she loved me the same. But the love that she fostered for me, as an agent of sustainable change in the Black community, had not wavered. Some may say love is love – but one who has not been the object of love this transitional could not ascertain the differing facets of this love experience, therefor one could not fathom the pain that was concomitant with this fact.

One form of love was personal, the other form impersonal. The personal form excited passions and desires in me for her. The impersonal form excited compassion, intense respect and honor in me – for the support that she afforded my cause. Though both resulted in intense emotion, their application was different and separate.

They could exist simultaneously or individually, and though I'd in the past, been blessed to experience their simultaneous application through her, that application in my mind, had become painfully individualistic.

This fact procured in me an urgency which I used as fuel to perpetuate my work ethic. I continued to write feverishly, finishing my urban fiction "Street Poisoned" in 60 days and submitted it for publishing. I asked my comrade Evil to critique the book and write a review that would be printed on the back page of the book. I wanted someone who had lived the Structural Gang Culture© experience, rather than an uninformed critic to write the review – for it was our experience that I was articulating. Evil obliged.

Chapter Twenty

In October of 2008, I filed my 1983 Civil Complaint, Case No. C08-1430-MJP, against Department of Corrections staff, and thought the court dismissed the Complaint against seven of the defendants, it allowed the Complaint to advance against nine of the remaining defendants.

December came quickly and the day for oral arguments in **Le'Taxione® v. The State of Washington** was upon us. Myisha attended the oral arguments so I anxiously awaited her perspective, as an attorney, on the results. When we spoke, she was very upbeat and optimistic about the outcome. She praised Jeff Ellis's representation of me. Mr. Ellis had an unassuming quality as it related to his appearance, but when he opened his mouth to speak, his experiential and instructional knowledge of the law poured forth so abundantly, that one could easily mistake it for arrogance – and I loved it.

She'd relayed that Jeff extinguished every aspect of the prosecutor's argument and that it was obvious that Jeff was better prepared and that fact was acknowledged in the Judges' facial expressions, demeanors, and follow-up questions they posed to the prosecutor.

"Are you saying, Prosecutor, that this man should not even be given an Evidentiary Hearing to ascertain the veracity of his claims?" one of the Judges asked.

Approximately ten days later, I received a letter, via legal mail, from Jeff Ellis. When I got the letter, I was sort of apprehensive and even fearful of its contents, but I opened and read it. In essence, it referred my case back to the Superior Court for an Evidentiary Hearing to ascertain the veracity of my claim – that I was not notified of my collateral attack rights. This was one of the exceptions to the time bar.

If I could prove in an Evidentiary Hearing that I hadn't been notified of my collateral attack rights which, in essence, informed me that in accord with RCW 10.73.090, I had one year to challenge my conviction. My court date was scheduled for late February of 2009. I was ecstatic.

Myisha informed me that she wanted to go back to school to get her PhD. Though I was happy for her, I knew what that entailed. She would not be able to help me with N'STEP® as she had in the past, for the time that she did have would have to be spent studying in order to make her dreams a reality. I felt abandoned. I felt deceived. I felt betrayed. How could she do this to me? She knows that the recidivism rate is directly related to one's inability to secure gainful employment. N'STEP® was the vision that would allow me to exact my salvation, atonement, and redemption through serving the Structural Gang Culture© and the community.

I didn't have the luxury of gaining my liberation and returning to society without the innovative and vibrant opportunity that N'STEP® presented me with. Though I knew that N'STEP® would suffer in its production of material, she, Myisha, also had the inalienable right to pursue her vision and it was selfish of me to even entertain the thoughts of abandonment and betrayal. In light of this revelation, I would discontinue the N'STEP® newsletter and make "Street Poisoned" my last publication, in my attempt to show my support for the decision that she'd made, so I thought.

Chapter Twenty-One

February of 2009 came, and I was transferred back to the Pierce County Jail for my Evidentiary Hearing. While there, I saw numerous brothers that I'd done time with who'd been released but were now on their way back to the prison with fresh beefs (new cases).

I sat in my assigned cell and pondered the determinates that not only facilitated, but also perpetuated recidivism and I found that 95% of men and women who are incarcerated across America will be released back into society, a very small percentage of them have addressed the issues that procured their incarceration – and even a modicum of that percentage had the normalcy that the family structure provides to those being released back into society.

Men whom had, prior to being incarnated, low self-esteem, a distorted perception of themselves, and an immature concept of manhood – which informed misogynistic and degrading views of women – making them abusers of the feminine principle of life – and while incarcerated – nurtured those views, returned to society, and continued to be the womanizers that they were prior to incarceration. That destroys any chance of cultivating family, which is the basis of a vibrant community.

I refused to nurture that in myself. I'd been a disrespecter of the feminine principle of life prior to incarceration. I'd promised God that I would never entertain life on such a base level again. The woman that I chose to love, I would spend the rest of my life with. We would make our intentions to be one in accord with God's law, making our vows sacred through the vehicle of marriage.

My court day arrived and upon entering, I saw Myisha, as beautiful as ever, and silently thanked God for her. Mr. Ellis came over to speak with me at which time he notified me that the prosecutor had not shown up. He then asked, "if I would like to stay in county jail or return to the prison to wait for our rescheduled Hearing, which would be set for March 2009."

I chose to return to the prison. That evening, Myisha came to visit me in the county jail. I'd not seen her for approximately a year before my court date and I fell in love with her all over again during our visit. She was so precious, so special, so beautiful, so woman.

We talked, we laughed and just enjoyed one another. She meant the world to me and was so essential in my growth as a man. She, in her daily rotation, gave me so much knowledge of woman and the vastness of her essence, that I was nostalgic in her presence. She was the very essence of what womanhood was, but she was plagued by the trauma of her past, just as I was.

While in transport back to CBCC, I pondered my imminent liberation and a life lived on a level of which I've never experienced. I pondered the small things such as shopping, taking out the garbage, and just laying with Myisha while watching a movie. These are the things that intrigued my heart and brought joy to an otherwise grim circumstance.

I'd been transferred to the Washington State Corrections Center in lieu of being returned to CBCC. The experience was reminiscent of when I was first committed to the Department of Corrections, without the despair of a life without the possibility of parole sentence.

Chapter Twenty-Two

When I arrived at CBCC, I was taken through the rigma-role of being processed all over again. "At least I don't have to go back through the D-Unit experience", I reasoned. I got back to my assigned cell. My Comrade Evil was authentically happy to see me. His eyes lit up at the sight of me, as did mine. I'd missed my comrade and he'd missed me.

"What happened Homie?" Evil asked.

"The prosecutor didn't show up, so they rescheduled me for late March", I replied.

"They know they lost, Homie, so they are going to try to drag you out", Evil said.

"Without a doubt! But the delay won't change the outcome. The God had already sanctioned my liberation from this present circumstance and His decree never leaves His mouth and returns without effectuating the change that He's ordained", I replied.

Over the next several days, Evil and I spoke of effective ways in which he could invest and draw benefit from while simultaneously serving the community. We'd already held positions in the institution's Cultural Unity Organization (CUO), wherein I was Vice President and he was the Sgt. Of Arms. We were planning our yearly Juneteenth celebration. Our only problem was that because our groups sponsor was an officer, he couldn't separate himself from the penological objective, and, how could he? These were the people who were issuing him the checks, making it possible for him to sustain himself.

Our sponsor, C/O Grimes, had an interpersonal relationship with the President of our CUO group that the body was not privy to. They held confidential meetings out of the presence of the board, which sparked suspicion within the body. This fact disallowed trust and confidence and undermined the integrity of the board. Perpetuating a perception of duplicity and complicit compromise under the tutelage of an administration that was hostile to our agenda, which was to raise the consciousness of Afrikan Americans behind the steel curtains of the Prison Industrial Complex.

I couldn't grove the unsavory nature of the interpersonal relationship that existed between Zirconia, our President, and C/O Grime, so I continued to follow the instructions delegated to me by Zirconia.

Evil had expressed his interest in production music, but he had not the support needed to make this a reality. I informed him that N'STEP® had, in the past, assisted the incarcerated persons in the realization of their goals. N'STEP® has participated in youth violence marches, had been one of the sponsors of the Black Panther Party's 41st annual celebration, had provided hygiene articles for the incarcerated, and had even paid for an attorney for an Afrikan brother named Kumdack Deng – who did not have a clear understanding of the English language which hindered his understanding of his case.

I informed Evil that if he wrote to N'STEP®, delineating his goals clearly, that the N'STEP® CEO may approve his funds which would assist him in the purchase of some equipment that would allow him to further his goals.

Evil wrote to N'STEP®, the funds were approved, and he was able to purchase a beat machine. After receiving his beat machine, Evil began, in earnest, making beats and interviewing prison artists for his project, which was a compilation CD featuring the best rappers and R&B singers in the facility.

While making beats in our assigned cell, we came up with the idea to make a CD soundtrack for my first urban fiction "Street Poisoned", and give it away free with purchase of the book.

There, behind the sullen gray walls, under the oppression of a cell, the soundtrack to a book was born.

Chapter Twenty-Three

I continued to litigate my Civil Complaint against the Department of Coercion (Corrections). Evil continued making his compilation CD, and in the midst of it all in early March of 2009, Gangology 101©: The New Paradigm (N'STEP's 2nd Edition) was published. I was very excited about the publication of Gangology 101© - for it encompassed both the psychological and sociological dynamics that perpetuated the violent Structural Gang Culture© mentality advancing a multi-pronged strategy of "Engaging the Youth, Changing the Future®."

Before I knew it, it was time for me to return to Pierce County Jail for my Evidentiary Hearing in Superior Court. I packed and found myself once again in transit. It just so happened this time that the President for the CUO, Zirconia, was too, returning to Pierce County Jail to be resentenced. He had been unjustly sentenced under the Three Strikes Law wherein he received a sentence of Life Without the Possibility of Parole.

As Zirconia and myself sat on the Blue Goose (transit bus) with out ankles, wrists, and waists chained – I decided that I would use the time to check his temperature (see what was on his mind).

"What's going down between you and C/O Grimes?" I cracked.

"What do you mean?" Zirconia replied.

"Members of the board and myself have concerns about the secrecy in which C/O Grimes and yourself interact", I said.

"You know, not everything that we discuss is not for the body to hear", Zirconia said.

That statement was very revealing in and of itself, but I kept mining for the information needed to ascertain his veracity or lack thereof.

"What makes you believe that veiled conversations between yourself and staff are something that are not to be conveyed to the body?" I asked.

"Some of the things we discuss have nothing to do with the CUO", he replied.

"If it has nothing to do with the CUO, the conversation should not take place. You're in position of President. You can't even allow the perception of an impropriety, for to do so eradicates the confidence of the body in its leadership and then this renders us impotent", I stated.

I saw that our conversation had become of interest to the rest of those being transported so I suggested that we table the discussion for another time outside the earshot of spectators. Zirconia agreed.

After arriving at WCC, Zirconia and myself were separated, and though we were both transported to Pierce County, he was transported the next day. I would be forced to wait for my transport. This worked to my benefit, for the next day at gym I saw my nephew London. I hadn't seen London since he was approximately 8 years old and I'd heard through the grapevine that the streets reported that he'd been shot several times by the Lakewood Police.

London was now 21 years old and very tall and skinny.

"Yo-Yo!" someone screamed.

I turned to see where the voice had come from. The last person I expected to see behind the steel curtains was London. I looked directly into the face of this young, tall brother and I couldn't place his face... London, seeing that I was searching my mind for his identity said, "It's London."

I flashed a smile so big that my face noticed the overextension. Words can never explain the plethora of emotions that I'd experienced within seconds of recognizing my nephew, but just as I washed with joy, sadness pursued on its heels. My nephew was locked up, and I regarded this fact with a tearful spirit. I remembered all of the times that I'd implored my nephew to not fall prey to the criminal just-us (justice) system, while simultaneously brandishing the gangster lifestyle that I warned him against.

"What's up London?" I excitedly asked. I didn't even wait for him to respond before I advanced my line of questioning.

"I heard that you'd been shot by the police", I stated.

"Yes, but I'm good", London replied.

Just then, an officer stated, "You can't be talking to the other unit."

"I'll get at you!" I stated to London and went to the gym to work out.

I was surprised that London exhibited the same love for me that he'd exhibited as a child. I had been made cognizant of the fact that his mother had told them I'd killed his stepfather. Though this was a blatant prevarication, a child hearing it from his mother, in most instances, would have tainted the image of the object of the prevarication, but London knew me, for even after the murder of his stepfather, he'd spent a great deal of time with me and my son.

He knew that the love he experienced with me could not have been fabricated, and for it to have been fabricated, would meant that

I was a cold-blooded killer. Contrary to popular belief, I was not a cold-blooded killer. Of course, I perpetuated unrestrained violence in the advancement of my Hood, under the "Doctrine of Retaliation©", but that was mandated by the lifestyle that I lived and the environment that I lived in. I was no more of a killer than anyone else acting out of the trauma concomitant with the reality and Commercial Transmission© of the Structural Gang Culture© mentality.

London loved me, and it showed in his excitement to see me. As I worked out, my mind raced from past to present, taking into account nothing in the interim. I couldn't grasp all that had happened in the 12-plus years since I'd been apprehended. I was here and now, in the progressive progress to secure my liberation, against all odds. Regardless of what London's mother had told him, it was my turn, and perceptions of me were miniscule in the grand scheme of things.

Chapter Twenty-Four

I was shackled, chained, and put on the transport bus headed for Pierce County. When I arrived, I was taken through the same booking process that I'd went through 13 years prior when I first fought my case. I was fingerprinted, had my photo taken, and then placed in the booking room.

I immediately called Myisha who was on her way to work. She was very happy to hear that I was in the county jail. This was just one more step in the process of securing my total liberation from my present circumstance. Our conversation was very upbeat and the circumstances under which we were conversing were surreal.

After touching base with Myisha, I sat waiting to be assigned a cell upstairs. After a couple of hours, I was assigned a single cell in 3- West, which was not an open module. In 3-West, you were only allowed out of your assigned cell for four hours a day, but that allotted time was more than I was allotted at CBCC. We were allotted three house a day in Closed Custody where I'd spent all of my time incarcerated, to the exception of the many years that I'd done in the Intensive Management Units (IMU's) at various facilities.

Once I got to the module, I could see that there were some people out of their assigned cells, and looking into the module, I could see that after 13 years, nothing had changed. Even the paint seemed the same. As I walked into the module, I could see that the men that were in the dayroom had not taken good care of themselves while in society. Everyone seemed malnourished and the brothers had a grayish tint to their skin. This was the effects of street life and concomitant drug culture.

Everyone was so small in comparison to me, as if their growth had been stunted, and gauging their conversation in passing, I could tell that their developmental process had been aborted to the point that their arrest was not only physical, but it was also psychological, educational, and emotional. When I got to my assigned cell, I immediately made my bunk and began going over my legal work. I was deep into my transcripts when I heard, "Is that Le'Taxione®?"

This had to be someone that I knew or who'd known me while doing time and I welcomed the familiarity.

"The one and only! Who is that?" I yelled back.

"It's Nutty from 6-0", he returned.

Nutty was one of the Crips that I'd done time with at Walla Walla. He'd been sentenced to Life as a youth and had been down (incarcerated) for at least 17 years. A change in the law presented him with the rare opportunity to be re-tried or resentenced. The last that I'd heard of him was that he went back to court, posted an appeal bond, and was free.

"West up, Nutty?" I asked.

"I'll be out in a minute. I'm going to come down and holler at you", Nutty replied.

"Without a doubt!" I answered and returned to my transcripts.

I would be testifying under oath at my evidentiary hearing and this was no light matter. Though the truth of my case was evident, it behooved me to overstand every angle in which the prosecutor would advance to attempt to discredit my testimony. I would once again be faced with that secret society called the Judicial System but this time, I was prepared. I'd studied the case inside and out for the past 13 years, and knowing what I knew now, they would not talk over my head as I sat too ignorant to ask questions and defend myself, which was the case in my first trial. In addition, I had retained, arguably, one of the best attorneys in the Northwest, whom I trusted with my life, and in all reality, this was in no stretch of the imagination, about my life… literally.

Nutty came to my assigned cell smiling ear to ear. After we exchanged greetings, he asked what was going on in my case. I gave him the short version of the scenario then inquired about his reincarceration.

"I came back on appeal and bonded out. I was out there working, but my paycheck didn't sustain the bare minimum cost of living, which led me to selling ecstasy pills. The cat that was supplying me turned out to be the Feds (Snitch) and when I went to make my last deal with him, they cracked me (arrested) me with $50,000 and 2,500 ecstasy pills, I'm facing federal time", Nutty said.

He too, had given me the short version of the scenario, and though it was the short version, it was the identical version that was told by every brother that came back to the pen. This was due to a lack of preparation while incarcerated and testament to the fact that a G.E.D. and plethora of self-help programs that incarcerated people are ran through, like products on an assembly line, does not give the individual the tools needed to matriculate back into society and be successful.

In fact, while witnessing the manner in which prison self-help programs are administered first hand, I'd long ago come to the conclusion that said programs were more about prison staff being afforded the opportunity to supplement their own incomes by facilitating these programs, rather than truly affording the incarcerated person the skills needed to successfully re-integrate back into society. There had to be curriculum which incorporated a trauma-based theory in order to truly effectuate change within the individual, which in turn, empowers him/her in a manner that gives them the inner strength to resist the synthetic ideology of instant gratification and all of its trappings.

Nutty and I reminisced about the time that the California Car (those incarcerated in Washington who were from California) almost went to war behind him taking food from a cat's tray in the Chow-Hall at WSP. We got a laugh out of that incident in hindsight and in that moment in time, the intensity of our present circumstance was lightened... for that brief moment in time.

Chapter Twenty-Five

The next day, Jeff came to visit me to brief me on the procedure that governed evidentiary hearings. For only the second time in two year, I sat across from the man that had done for me more in two years, what attorneys had failed to do in thirteen years, and that was to get me back in court. Jeff sat very regally on the other side of the table from me in a very small room used for attorney visits. He briefed me on the procedure of an evidentiary hearing. He informed me that our task was to prove that I was not verbally notified of my collateral attack rights on the record during the sentencing, in accord with RCW 10.73.090, which would be easy because the transcripts reflected this fact. Providing that I was not notified of my collateral attack rights would prohibit the courts from arbitrarily exercising the one-year time frame which the prosecutor argued in attempt to negate my right to litigate for my liberation at this point in my sentence.

Jeff also made cognizant of the fact that my previous Habeas attorney, Leslie Stomsvik, who'd taken $12,000 from me to represent me in this case, but in fact misrepresented me, and was admonished by the Washington State Bar Association for doing so, would be called as a witness for the prosecution to testify as to when I'd received my Judgement and Sentencing documents, which expressed an illegal, permissive form of my collateral attack rights. My trial attorney, Hari Alipuria, would also take the stand on my behalf to verify that he had no recollection of me being notified on the record or by any document of my collateral attack rights.

After Jeff and I finished the briefing, we exchanged pleasantries and terminated the meeting, but not before I mentioned The God and our Lord and Savior Jesus Christ's intervention in our cause. Jeff smiled and we parted company.

I returned to the module where Nutty immediately questioned me concerning my attorney visit. I told him what I wanted him to know and changed the subject. Once inside my assigned cell, I contemplated the possibilities of my life, and the long journey that led to the people that became distinct in this event. As I searched my mind, I found that not one of the members of my family were involved, not even remotely, in my endeavor to secure my liberation. Though this fact was not lost on me, it did not enrage me, for it was the norm.

Countless men, women, and children languish in the penal system and are treated by their families as if they didn't exist. This has become a societal norm as it applied to black people who disproportionately populated the penal system. According to the Department of Justice statistics, Afrikan Americans made up 13.5% of the population in America, but were over 65% of the prison population.

I guess the reason why the Scales of Justice are tilted in the symbolic picture of the Lady of Justice is because she's peeking out from under her blindfold. I changed my thoughts and began doing California Burpees (calisthenics) vigorously in an attempt to regain focus on my evidentiary hearing which would be held the following day.

Chapter Twenty-Six

The next day, I awakened at my usual 4:30 a.m. I felt very well rested and vibrant. I brushed my teeth, washed my face, and got dressed, after which I read scripture, then prayed. After praying, I began reading over my case, familiarizing myself with the language and the concepts that were espoused therein. The law was clearly on my side and at my disposal which moved me to ponder the concept of justice and lack thereof in my case.

Justice demands that the punishment be commensurate to the crime. Here I'd languished for 13 years under a sentence of Life Without the Possibility of Parole (Three-Strikes), when my criminal history demanded, at the maximum, 75 months. I was forced out of introspection by the lights being turned on in the module. It was time for breakfast. The sheriff opened the food slot on my assigned cell door and pushed my tray through. I sat on the slab of concrete that the two-inch mattress lay on, serving as my bunk. Due to dietary laws, I didn't accept the tray. I'd long practiced eating one meal a day for spiritual and health reasons. That one meal would be in the times of 6-8 p.m.

In my stay behind those steel curtains, I'd watched the brothers' appearances were transformed by their diets. I'd found that those who could not exercise restraint in their intake of food could not exercise restraint in other aspects of their demonstration. The two deepest drives in Man are food and sex. Whichever one of these drives that he cannot control, that's the one that becomes his God. I disciplined both.

After the trays were received, I was permitted to take a shower in preparation for court. The shower felt more like spiritual purification. As I stood under the water, it was as if all cares had been washed away and I experienced a calm and peace that surpassed overstanding. A calm and peace that came directly from The God. After the cleansing, I returned to my assigned cell, sat on the bunk, and smiled out loud.

Nutty came to the cell to encourage me on the outcome of my hearing. As he spoke, my mind traveled 24 million miles per second. Though he was trying to support me, as a comrade, I felt sorrow for him and his newfound circumstance. I didn't wish incarceration on my worst enemy and here was a brother that I genuinely liked, that after 17 or 18 years and a very short stint of freedom, was back in the belly of the beast. I was notified by the sheriff that other sheriffs were on their way to escort me to court.

"Good luck, Homie", Nutty said.

"Luck is when preparation meets opportunity and I've long prepared for this opportunity", I cracked as I left the module.

I was let into a hallway where other incarcerated men were standing, who too, were being escorted to court. We were all handcuffed to one long chain and led down the hall in route to the various courtrooms where our attempts to secure our liberation would be granted or denied.

At that moment, the smell of the hall, the clinking of the chains, and the eerie silence of the men became magnified and reminiscent of the time that I first traversed these halls and the resultant life sentence, but this time it would be the diametric opposite.

"This time I will secure my liberation", I reasoned.

As we were traveling down the last stretch of the hallway that led to the courtroom that I was scheduled to appear in, two young brothers were coming in the opposite direction, both in suits, which meant they were either in trial or had finished trial.

"Hold your head youngstas", I said as they passed.

It was obvious to me that they needed that inspiration at that very moment and that I'd given it to them, for they raised their heads simultaneously and said, "That's right!" in unison. Later on I would learn that they were sentenced to Life Without.

Chapter Twenty-Seven

I walked into the courtroom and quickly panned the audience, and there sat Myisha and her mother, the only two people interested in enough in my liberation to attend the hearing. I flashed a smile at Myisha as she mouthed the words, I love you. The interaction between Myisha and myself had become strained to say the least, but I, (ML) kept pushing N'STEP® agenda with the urgency that it demanded. In my mind, she was not the friend to me that she'd been in the past and though she attempted to mask this fact with what I perceived to be fabricated spurts of interest in my work, I could tell it wasn't like it used to be. (ML). I had no time to dwell on these facts.

What was imperative was that I stay in perpetual motion and that's what I did. I was ushered into the courtroom, shackled, and sat in the jury box where other men were already sitting, waiting to address their concerns with Judge Tollifson. While waiting, we witness the re-sentencing of an Asia man who'd come back on appeal due to irregularities in his sentence. The scenario would have been of no interest to me – except that in this re-sentencing, Judge Tollifson initiated the procedure dictated by RCW 10.73.090 by notifying the defendant of his collateral attach rights on the record and then having him sign his notice of collateral attack forms, procedure that was not followed in my case and was, in fact, one of the reasons why I was back in court for an evidentiary hearing.

I looked to Jeff to see if he'd recognized what transpired before our eyes. He returned a look of acknowledgement and nodded ever so slightly. After the Asia man had been re-sentenced, I was called and escorted to a long table in front of the Judge's bench. Jeff immediately went into action.

"Your Honor, I would my client, Le'Taxione®, to be uncuffed for this proceeding."

Judge Tollifson quickly addressed the bailiff, "Is there a reason that Mr. Le'Taxione® is handcuffed"

"Well, Your Honor, this is procedure, but I'll call my supervisor to see if he can be uncuffed", the bailiff replied.

While the bailiff made his call, the prosecutor slipped out of the courtroom, came back in abruptly, and motioned to Jeff. Jeff then walked outside of the courtroom with the prosecutor. I know what you're thinking because some of you have been in this position, but I had total confidence in my attorney. Jeff returned and informed me that my previous attorney, Leslie Stomsvik was out in the hall and in his opinion, he was not at all credible. I saw, in Jeff's eyes, an instant dislike for the position Mr. Stomsvik was taking on behalf of the prosecutor, but I also saw his confidence that whatever Mr. Stomsvik said, he would go after him without reticence, and I loved seeing Jeff like that.

The bailiff was obviously told to uncuff me because he did. Jeff expressed to me his antipathy for the fact that I was cuffed, but what was alarming, in hindsight, I'd been cuffed for so long behind these steel curtains that it bothered Jeff more than it bothered me. This was a testament to how environment and its norms can shape one's perception to the point where an injustice, if experienced on a continuum, becomes inherently acceptable.

There is no one who exits the prison experience and is not affected in one way or another. It is geared, in it's daily application, to subvert humanness and introduced one to the mentality of a slave, so it is written in the Thirteenth Amendment of the U.S. Constitution that: Neither slavery nor involuntary servitude, except as punishment for a crim, whereof the party shall have been convicted, shall exist in the United States. So, though slavery was abolished in 1863, it was written into the Constitution and cloaked in the above language. Imagine that.

The evidentiary hearing began, and Jeff came out swinging. Among other things, he credited the Judge for exhibiting the proper manner in which the Judge gave the previous defendant his notice of collateral attack rights on the record and on paper. Then he showed through the testimony of my previous attorney, the deputy prosecutor at the time I was sentenced, and myself, that this didn't happen in my case. Then, the prosecutor did something strange, she rested her case. I smiled out loud.

Judge Tollifson refused to publish his decision that day, so he rescheduled the hearing for the next week, at which time, he would publish his decision.

Chapter Twenty-Eight

I returned to my assigned module optimistic about my attorney's performance. Upon returning, I found Nutty waiting for me.

"What happened, Homie?" Nutty asked.

"I got to go back to court next week, I won't know until then", I said.

It seemed as if the pure evanescence of time was made manifest in this circumstance because before I was aware of it, my court day was at hand. I was again escorted down the very same hallways that I traveled in my initial conviction in this case, and, once again, I was at peace concerning the outcome. Coming through the courtroom doors, I looked to my left and the Myisha sat. I flashed a smile and then was seated next to Jeff at the table. Jeff was again perturbed about the fact that I was shackled.

Soon after I'd been seated, Judge Tollifson made his entrance and, in accord with court decorum, we stood and were again seated as he took his seat on the bench. He began, "In the matter of Le'Taxione® v. State of Washington, Case No. 97-1-04547-1, I adopt the Petitioner's findings of fact with one correction", Judge Tollifson said.

The adoption of my findings of fact meant that I was correct in my assertion that I was not orally or by document of my collateral attack rights in accord with RCW 10.73.090, therefore, the one year time frame did not apply to me and now my case must be heard by the Court of Appeals on the merits. As the excitement of this major win coursed through my veins, Judge Tollifson began speaking again.

"I also find that the defendant was given his Judgement and Sentencing."

This was a blatant attempt to give the prosecutor something that she could use to neutralize my victory, because the Judgement and Sentencing document mentions collateral attack rights, though they are not described in accord with RCW 10.73.090. Even in the adoption of the findings of fact, the incestuous nature of this secret society labeled "the justice system" undermined the integrity of the process.

In essence, the Judge ruled for and against me in the same breath, but I knew the fact that he adopted our findings of fact was enough to procure the relief required because said RCW governing notification specifically states that "a defendant shall be notified on the record during sentencing of his/her collateral attack rights.

Jeff was visually dismayed at the ruling by the Judge, but I was peace. As I rose from my seat to be escorted back to my assigned module, I looked into Myisha's face. She was disheartened and perplexed. In my perception, she'd long lost faith in this process, but continued in case everything worked out. Here interest in my work had waned. This was made evident by her reactions to my accomplishments. At one time, she's be ecstatic with my completion and publication of curricula and books, but now all that these accomplishments garnered was a rote and lackluster congratulations, but I didn't allow this to deter me. How could I?

That which was evident reiterated itself in my conscious thought, informing me that, regardless of how one reacts to your work, it is your salvation, your atonement... your redemption. I returned to CBCC, ecstatic about my victory. I had not the time nor energy to feed doubt. I knew that The God had destined me for greater things that I'd chosen for myself, but in reality, one cannot compel another to see nor invest in what The God has shared with him. He can only stay the course and let his work speak for him.

Chapter Twenty-Nine

I returned to CBCC and all that it implied. The same racism, the same discrimination, and the same rogue officers, and the same adverse and contentious discourse between Myisha and I. In my travels to and from court N'STEP®'s 2nd Edition, Gangology 101©: The New Paradigm had been published and I'd finally gotten a copy in my hands. I was so very proud of the material and its transformational properties.

I'd been in contact with my Comrade, Randy "Blue Bear" Dixon, sporadically, and upon return from court, I called to inform him of my legal victory as well as the publication of Gangology 101©. Blue was one of my staunchest supporters and he created covers for my work prior to Gangology 101©. He was authentically elated at the news. We discussed the issues that were prevalent in Fresno amongst the Structural Gang Culture© and how these issues ignited the Doctrine of Retaliation©.

We continued to plan our assault on the "miscreant aspects of the gang mentality©", but I could hear in his voice that he was becoming more despondent concerning the state of our youth in Fresno, so I extended to him comfort and hope through both my analysis of, and panacea for the issue. During our discourse, Blue advanced the idea that we'd discussed previously, and that was me writing a children's book. I was hesitant to take on this project at this particular time because I was meeting so much opposition from Myisha when it came to creating a body of work.

Not that she didn't want me to, but due to the fact that she was pursuing her PhD., though (PM) Myisha expressed enthusiasm about me writing a children's book, she had no time to do the work necessary to actualize the publication of my work, and this fact, in many ways, decimated aspects of my creativity.

After extracting from Blue, the promise that he would create the images needed to publish the children's book, we exchanged our love for one another and ended our discourse. I began working on the children's book entitled "I AM MORE THAN A GANG MEMBER©."

In the interim, I'd found that rogue C/O's at CBCC were a part of a motorcycle gang called the "Roughnecks". I say gang because the Department of Justice describes a gang as three or more individuals who wear the same clothes, exhibit criminal behavior, and create an atmosphere of fear and intimidation (paraphrased). These C/O's represented the same colors, signs, flags, symbolism, they exhibited criminal behavior in their arbitrary and capricious confiscation of my legal work during cell searches and created and atmosphere of fear and intimidation through their retaliatory tactics of planting razor blades in men's assigned cells if they filed grievances against them.

I'd filed to the federal courts trying to get a preliminary injunction against C/O's in my 1983 Civil Complaint, Case No. C08-1430-MJP, for illegally confiscating my legal work during cell searches, but my motion was denied, and the Complaint that I'd filed to the head of the Department of Corrections in the State of Washington, not taking into account Officers Cram's and Dufuss's criminal behavior, was answered, but advanced that said motorcycle gang was in fact a non-profit organization and that, though I'd filed numerous grievances about this issue, there was no sufficient evidence to substantiate my claims.

How could there be when the same administration that condones this "Fifth Column" in their midst are the ones that are conducting the so-called investigation of my Complaint. I continued my work, not allowing these facts to deter me.

Chapter Thirty

All motions and replies concerning my evidentiary hearing had been submitted. Now, my case was on the Washington State Appellate Court's desk waiting to be decided on its merits.

I finished the context of the children's book in 40 days. Now, I had to wait for my Comrade Blue to finish the water-colored images that he was creating for the book. He created 24 images and a cover for the book, which depicted three primary characters of the book; one of whom had painted the picture of our First Black President, Barack Obama, on the wall.

The concept was my way of honoring President Obama for the intelligence and integrity he exhibited in his bid to become President. Obama's Presidency was not only historic, but it was validating and uplifting. I'd hoped that the fact that we now had a Black President would ease race relations in America and it seemed, in the beginning, to do just that, but this new found harmony was experienced only among the youth and was short-lived.

Racism was agitated and couldn't accept a Black man as the President. This fact made itself manifest as the status quo's opposition to everything that Obama proposed from stimulus packages to stimulate and inherited failed economy, to health care for all. I wrote an article in the N'STEP® Newsletter entitled "President Barack

Obama: Confirmation, Inspiration, and Indictment", that read:

President Barack Obama:
Confirmation, Inspiration, and Indictment

First and foremost, we must congratulate our President, Barack Obama, not only for winning the presidential election, but also for introducing a bipartisan, universal politic that transcends America's historically partisan antics and lack of transparency that left the populous in the dark concerning our government's activities.

While many, including Afrikan Americans, celebrate the fact that we have a Black President, we must pay close attention to the dispensation of time that we've entered and what that time dictates as it applies to our activities as Black men in particular. President Obama's position as Commander and Chief is **CONFIRMATION**, for it in many ways validates what our community advocates, activists, and revolutionaries have spent their lives saying, which is that a Black man, if given the same opportunity, can govern the most powerful country in the world.

It is **INSPIRATION**, for it gives Black men a level of excellence to which they can aspire as opposed to the mere sports, entertainment, criminality, and miscreance that we've been pigeonholed into and even encouraged to pursue.

It is **INDICTMENT**, for even though it does not in and of itself eradicate the cancer of racism prevalent in America, it nullifies the archaic, self-defeatist excuses we as Black men have often adopted and still use to justify our sedentary work ethic.

It is **INDICTMENT**, for it reiterates and substantiates the importance of family, community and nation: re-connecting those who have felt prohibited from accessing the American value system, back to this country, it's plight, and our individual responsibility to the possibility of its greatness.

It is **INDICTMENT**, for it ignites the responsibility of true fatherhood, giving many of us who have not experience the physical example, a prototype that we can aspire to, affording our children a litmus test by which to gauge our activities as fathers.

It is **INDICTMENT**, for it makes evident the true actualization of Black manhood, as opposed to the immature interpretation that is prevalent in our society and that which we've erroneously applied to our circumstance. The Presidency of Barack Obama and the present dispensation of time dictates that we as Black men recognize, identify and transcend© the current mentality that condones, rationalizes and justifies our lackluster approach to life, liberty and success. It compels us to engage in a preparatory process that will allow us to matriculate into the President's administration through our reformation in order to transform our families, communities, and nation.

We salute you Mr. President!

I was proud of my President, but I experienced the backlash of his Presidency

As every black man in America did. In the summer 2009, my first urban fiction, "STREET POISIONED", was published and I was featured in the California-based wheels magazine's 45th issue. In October of 2009, my children's book, "I AM MORE THAN A GANG MEMBER", was submitted for publishing. Blue had done an excellent job on the water-color images for the book. They were descriptive, vibrant, and I was very proud of his work.

Blue had been teaching the N'STEP® process out of his home in Fresno, California, ad every time that I'd put down a new book, he'd sit some of the young comrades down and they'd read from the newly published material. He'd already decided the fascination that young comrades exhibited when reviewing the material. They were intrigued by the fact that I'd accomplished what I had from behind these steel curtains. That, in and of itself, made evident that it is not your circumstance that dictates your productivity. On the contrary, it is your productivity, or lack thereof, that dictates your circumstance.

Chapter Thirty-One

N'STEP® had purchased a beat-box for my Comrade Evil and we began creating a soundtrack for the urban fiction to release, free of charge, with the book, "STREET POISIONED." To my knowledge, this had never been done and it made use of lyrics that I'd written at the time I was pursuing rap.

In November of 2009, I'd been informed that I was being promoted to a Medium Custody facility. I pondered the intentions that lie behind the veil of this promotion. I took into account the fact that the Cultural Unit Organization (CUO), which I'd served on the Board as the Vice-President, had in no small part, due to the financial assistance of N'STEP® and myself, effectuated a successful Juneteenth celebration.

The success of the Juneteenth celebration showed that there was the possibility for unity amongst CBCC's Afrikan American population, and the fact that one as disdained by the administration as myself, played a major role in that success, had to be unsettling. I'd ascertained evidence that proved our sponsor's complicity and undermining the efforts of the CUO and expressed this fact with the Board members, most of whom expressed the very same sentiments.

When said sponsor began speaking disparagingly about me to the members of the Gangster Disciple Nation in an attempt to create a hostile environment for me. It made my evidenced facts not only plausible, but valid. I also took into account the fact that I'd been aggressively pursuing documents through Public Disclosure concerning rogue officers' facility records of misconduct.

The promotion then made sense. "I was being promoted in order to be moved to a different area of this prison as a preventative measure, in an attempt to protect the flagrant misconduct of the rogue officers", I reasoned.

This move would separate me from the CUO sponsor, C/O Grimes and other officers that had been retaliating against me, and though I didn't want to leave my Comrade Evil, and was apprehensive about being assigned a cell outside of the intense confinement of Closed Custody for the first time in 13 years, I embraced the thought.

Later that month, four Lakewood Police Officers were slain by a brother who'd been released from the Pierce County Jail. According to news accounts, the brother entered a coffee shop and opened fire on the four officers, taking a gun from one, killing them all. The brother had expressed, while in the county jail, that he'd grown tired of being harassed by the police. His perceived injustice on the part of the police department and lack of process of redress left him feeling disempowered and emasculated. He natural result of injustice is violence and that the tool this brother used for redress. Whether he was right or wrong was of no import to him.

Vengeance had infected the depths of his heart, blinding him to reason, compelling him to act out of savagery that was superimposed, in his mind, by the magnitude of injustice that he was subjected to at the hands of the policemen.

Out of compassion for the policemen's families, I'd proposed a CUO fundraiser that would donate all its proceeds to the Policemen's

<u>Guild,</u> to be distributed to the families of the slain officers. That gesture was denied by CBCC's administration. How contradictory! I though. The donation of the funds to the slain officers' families would give incarcerated people an avenue by which to access and exercise their humanity and a chance to show society that everyone that are incarcerated are not animals that subscribe to the wholesale killing of law enforcement officers.

Upon deeper contemplation, I reasoned that there is no benefit in the Department of Corrections showing humanity of its captives. There is only benefit in the portrayal of the incarcerated as violent animals. In the latter portrayal lies funding.

Chapter Thirty-Two

December 15, 2009, which was my birthday, rolled around without the observation of anyone besides Evil and myself. Myisha wished me a Happy Birthday when I spoke with her. Our relationship was becoming more of a companionship as it absorbed the nefarious assaults wielded by distance and time. Whether advertently or inadvertently, consciously or subconsciously, she'd become secretive in her interaction. In some instances, she'd consciously chosen to keep secrets and when these circumstances were laid bare, she would cite fear of my reaction as an excuse for the secrecy.

There is no doubt that I could be curt at times in our discourse, but if it was, in fact, the abrasiveness of my reaction that she disdained, this was the same reasoning she should have prevailed on the front end of the decision, informing her decision to participate in anything that she felt would procure my curt response. My curtness was merely an effect commensurate to the secrecy, which was the cause. I did not overstand her premise of fear, for even in the midst of abrasive discourse, I've never used profanity or disrespected her in any manner.

So, disdain was based in traumatic experiences, yet that didn't make it unreal in her mind. The juxtaposition of her previous traumatic experiences, with my curt responses, in her mind, justified ad even exacerbated that disdain.

Knowing this, I began to temper my responses when that which was hidden was made manifest. I overstood how the trauma of past experiences informed present behavioral patterns and interaction, for I too, suffered from this reality, which could only be ameliorated by the Recognize, Identify, and Transcend© thought process espoused in the N'STEP® curriculum… at least for me.

Chapter Thirty-Three

December 2009 submitted to January 2010 without argument, and in January I was moved to a Medium Security facility, which was only separated from the Closed Custody facility by a few gates. Upon arriving, I decided that I didn't like the facility, but the reasons that I didn't like the facility were directly related to the fact that while in Closed Custody. I'd been trained to accept extended confinement and lack of institutional movement, so much so, that the free movement prevalent in Medium Custody was so foreign to me that it made me uncomfortable.

I felt out of place with the lack of restraint applied to my movement. I immediately selected an area in the dayroom away from the general population and occupied it daily. The only brother I knew in the module was a brother named Xavier. We'd met several times in passing but spoke extensively at the CUO's Juneteenth celebration. Xavier had been convicted of murder at the age of 15 and given a life sentence. He'd been incarcerated for 23 years at the time I moved into the module.

Can you imagine a child being sentenced to life at the age of 15, as if there could never be any reformation? The natural developmental process of the human being lends credence to the ability and chance to reform, yet this man, who was still a child in many ways, would not be given the chance to express his reformation in so-called free society, for a crime, wherein his mere presence garnered him a life sentence.

No other country sentences children life, subjecting them to the violence, concomitant with Institutional Confirmation©. I'd watched Xavier as he spoke to the President of the NAACP at our CUO Juneteenth celebration. As I measured the body language exhibited in their interaction, I knew that Mr. Bible, the President for the NAACP, was anything but a true activist. I'd surveilled his movements in the State of Washington for years, quickly assessing the fact that, if there were no cameras, there was no action on his behalf.

He'd spoken out on behalf of N'STEP® at one of the Black Prisoners Caucus (BPC) Summits , wherein I spoke on N'STEP® and the success that we'd had conducting a seven month long class at Monroe Correctional Complex (WSR/MCC) – but he'd only done so because, not only had the youth that were incarcerated asked why our second N'STEP® class was being prohibited by the WSR/MCC Administration, but there were two media cameras, media, and politicians at the Summit.

After the Summit, he went back to Nothing Accomplished After Considerable Pretense (NAACP) and I heard nothing from him again. After Xavier finished his dialogue with Mr. Bible, I went to the table to speak with him, at which time he relayed to me that Mr. Bible showed no interest in his circumstance, and at that moment, my heart cried.

I'd advanced the resolve of N'STEP® in helping Xavier actualize his freedom. He smiled, but I could tell his disappointment in Mr. Bible's position tainted his belief in my sincerity. We were now in the same module and I would make manifest my desire to aid and assist him.

The only other people that I knew at the Medium Security Facility was Dolla and Droopy. I'd met Dolla at WCC while in transport back to CBCC from court while at WCC. I'd watched Dolla for a couple of days and respected his demonstration. One day, while we were in the gym, I decided to approach him and introduce myself. As I walked across the room to do so, is eyes locked in on me. As I got closer to him, I could tell that he became apprehensive.

His body shifted and he prepared his feet for a possible attack. I knew what thoughts he was entertaining by reading his body language. Here I was, seasoned, and 220 lbs., very muscular, approaching an 18-year-old cat who weighed at that time, about a buck-sixty soaking wet with boots on. Upon approach I hit him with the Structural Gang Culture© introduction, "What Set that is?" (What Hood do you represent?)

"Gangster Disciple Folks", Dolla replied with all the bravado he could muster.

"This that Diamond Crips", I said as I extended my hand.

We shook hands, and at that moment, initiated a camaraderie that followed us to CBCC. As for the Comrade Droopy, our bond was less eventful. We were both from The Land and were both Crips. The love, respect, and honor was on sight.

Chapter Thirty-Four

Xavier and I began spending more time together. We grew closer and closer after every interaction. I became cognizant of the elements of the crime he was convicted of, which intensified my desire to see him free. "Yes, he deserved to do at least 20 years for his part in the crime, but he didn't deserve life", I reasoned. I placed at his disposal, myself and my resources, which were not plentiful, but they were significant. Though I sought Xavier's freedom in particular, I desired the freedom of all youth sentenced to life in this manner in general and I would employ N'STEP® to facilitate that desire.

I found myself not only engaged in a fight for my liberation, but now I also fought for the freedom of youths who had been sentenced to life. True greatness lies in the selfless pursuit of causes bigger than oneself. In February of 2010, my children's book "I AM MORE THAN A GANG MEMBER" was published. I marveled at its vibrant colors and professional format as I did with every publication of my work. It was one thing to write a book, but to have it published and in your hands was a separate aspect of that reality and this aspect is what brought me the most pleasure.

I had the N'STEP® organization forward the children's book to Blue for his collection and prolonged a call to him until I believed he'd received the book. I gave it approximately five days before I called him. When we did speak, he was elated and proud of our work. The images that he'd created for the book were vibrant and descriptive of the message conveyed in its text. I'd written a very special acknowledgement in the book, of Blue and the camaraderie we shared, not only in life, but also in the work that we'd done in our attempt to ameliorate the conditions that we'd both perpetuated through our violent escapades in our community.

Blue read my acknowledgement and became flustered. It was as if he'd not truly known how I felt about him an the assistance that he'd tendered to me throughout our lives as Diamond Boys, but now the whole world would know and maybe overstand that the fictive kinships created within the Structural Gang Culture© can evolve and be imperative in "Engaging the Youth...Changing the Future©."

Blue was one of my truest Comrades. So true, that we were more like brothers. He was true to our creed and never failed to aid and assist me. I held him in high esteem, as he did me. I wanted success for him, as he did for me. But, in all that want, we never forgot our duty to the Hood – and I will die in service to communities plagued by the miscreant aspect of the gang mentality© - and I will oppose all of those who represent themselves as instruments of change in our communities – but are in reality – blood-suckers of the poor who capitalize off the misery and exploit the Structural Gang Culture© by misappropriating funds made available to them to heal and revitalize our communities.

Chapter Thirty-Five

March came around and I met an older brother named Price. Mr. Price was also a victim of the Three-Strikes Law. He was also a chef. Mr. Price, Xavier and myself formed a bond that few people experience in a lifetime. Though I'd just met Mr. Price, he'd been in the module approximately six years. He'd left the facility for surgery and had come back in early March 2010. Xavier and Mr. Price had a friendship prior to me being assigned to that module and though we were all friends, on could tell that their relationship with each other was far more mature than the relationship that they had with me.

Though they did all they could to incorporate me into their friendship, I'd often experience the reality if being on the outside of their interaction, but time would negate this fact. I'd often times sit as they reminisced about the times that they'd shared and on occasion, erupt into laughter at their antics. I enjoyed their company and the meals that Mr. Price would cook were excellent.

I'll never forget how Short Legs (Xavier) would come out of his assigned cell early in the morning singing songs that forced my thoughts into pleasantries of my past experiences. Even though he could not carry a tune if it had a handle on it. Or how Mr. Price, at 65, would cut through the silence with his attempted rendition of a

Tupac rap, marred by forgotten words and misplaced phrases. These cats were funny. I remember one day Mr. Price was poking fun at Xavier by calling him Short Legs and Xavier replied, "They need someone to start the fire for the Sweat Lodge so you should be on the call-out so you can rub those fire-sticks you call legs together to start the fire."

I hit the floor laughing. From that day forward, Mr. Price was humorously known as Fire Starter. In mid-March 2010, I was called into the counselor's office. Once I got there, my counselor informed me that I had an attorney call. My heart immediately began pounding in my chest uncontrollably. When I got on the phone, I recognized the voice of my attorney's paralegal, a brother named Vance. Vance had been incarcerated with me at WSR and he had, in fact, introduced me to my attorney, Jeff Ellis. Vance too, had been sentenced to Three-Strikes, but had the sentence reversed on appeal. As a matter of fact, while speaking to Jeff concerning my case, he'd asked me to have Vance call him because he had won his appeal, so it was I who'd first informed Vance of his victory – which resulted in his Three-Strikes (Life Sentence) being overturned.

Upon me speaking into the phone, Vance stated, "Mr. Le'Taxione, you will be coming home. The appeal courts just vacated your sentence."

"That's what I'm talking about!" I yelled into the phone.

It was ironic that I'd been the one that notified him of his victory and two years later, he was the one that notified me of my victory. I hung up the phone, danced back into the module, and called Myisha. When I told her, she first screamed in disbelief, then began crying, repeatedly, saying "Thank you, Jesus. Thank you, Jesus. Thank you, Jesus."

Two days later I received my appeal back from the Court of

Appeals, dated March 9, vacating my sentence. This meant that I was no longer sentenced under the Three-Strikes law and that I would be returned to the county jail and re-sentenced to my standard range. I smiled out loud at the reality.

Can you imagine, after 13 years of a Life Without Parole sentence – winning your liberation. My standard range at its maximum was 75 months, which meant that I'd served seven years beyond my maximum. I read the Appellate Court's decision at least seven times. I was now free! All of my work and plans would not be actualized at the highest plane of its potential. I immediately pondered writing my next book, "Original Diamond Boy: The Transition".

Chapter Thirty-Six

Whem I spoke to Jeff, he congratulated me on the victory, but cautioned that the prosecutor had 20 days to file a "Motion for Reconsideration" and that he thought they would.

"But, we're in a better position because the Appellate Court, by majority, had ruled in our favor", Jeff stated.

"We're in a better position because The God is on our side!" I thought out loud and ended my conversation with Jeff and began my 20-day countdown. Xavier and Mr. Price were genuinely happy for me after hearing the news from the courts, but I could also see the sense of loss behind their smiles. We'd become very close, and even though they wanted me to be liberated from this circumstance, they hated to see me go.

The communication between Myisha and I had improved due to both of our conscious decisions to work on it, but it was only a matter of time before our communication broke down again. In the interim, the 20 days flew by. On the 20th day, the prosecution filed their "Motion for Reconsideration" and the Appeals Courts had 30 days to either grant their Motion or deny it.

Words would only trivialize the myriad of emotions that I experienced during the next 30 days. The anxiety, elation, and anger that I experienced were at times, overwhelming. I was in turmoil internally, but through prayer, I weathered the internal storm and stayed focused on my liberation. Another dynamic had been set in motion during this trial. Judas had arrived at the facility, but upon inspection, I found that he was not the same Comrade I once knew. As a matter of fact – his actions had become selfish and contrived. He sought the title of President for the CUO, the capacity that I'd already been acting in long before he arrived.

C/O Grimes, the CUO sponsor, saw Judas' aspirations and quickly moved to feed them by administering to the circumstance fabrications about me, giving rise to Judas' emotions, then directing them at his target…me. I didn't know how intricate the ploy of C/O Grimes had become, but in the ensuing months, I saw Judas' character change.

He began to miss class obtained by myself, wherein Afrikan Americans gathered and studied the plight of our People in America – wherein we brainstormed about effective panaceas that could be implicated to facilitate the justice that we weren't receiving at this racist facility – while remaining inside the parameters of the policies that governed our actions.

I didn't know how intricate and insidious C/O Grime's ploy had become, but I knew that it was directly related to how Judas had changed. Thirty days came and went with space-shuttle speed and I received in the mail the Appellate Court's decision on the prosecutor's Motion for Reconsideration. I opened the letter slowly, took out a single sheet of paper, which merely stated, Motion for Reconsideration DENIED.

This meant that the Court of Appeals had refused to give any credence to the prosecutor's Motion. Once again, I became celebratory, but it was not over. The prosecutor would have another 30 days to file a Motion for Discretionary Review to the Washington State Supreme Court. Now the 30-day countdown began all over again.

Chapter Thirty-Seven

On the last day of the prosecutor's 30-day time limit to file for a Discretionary Review to the Supreme Court – At 3:45 p.m. I called Jeff's office to see if the prosecutor had, in fact, filed their Motion. I got Vance on the phone, who informed me that the prosecutor, at that time, had not filed their Motion. This had serious implications. If the prosecutor did not file by the end of this business day, the case would be over, and I would be returned to court for resentencing.

I had to go to my assigned cell for count. "I'll call Vance after count", I reasoned. That hour it took to clear count seemed like another 30 days, easy. Count was over. I rushed out to the phone, but everyone had left the attorney's office for the day. "DAMN IT!" I yelled and slammed down the phone.

The next morning, I called, and Vance answered the phone. My heart began beating so loud that I heard it through my ears.

"Le'Taxione®, unfortunately the prosecution filed the Motion at 4:38 p.m., 22 minutes before their deadline."

Imagine that. I was 22 minutes away from liberation and they filed. Jeff immediately filed a cross Motion that also requested my immediate release, which was not addressed by the prosecutor. Once again, I was in suspended animation… at least as far as my legal battle was concerned – but I stayed in perpetual resistance.

Myisha and I continued to suffer from the inherent duplicity that encompasses any two people's desires to be as one, but the circumstance in which we found ourselves magnified our particular trials. We disagreed in her desire to be more active in the Church's functions, not because I was against the concept of serving the congregation, but because I abhorred the fact that the aspects of the Church's functions that she wanted to become more active in placed her out in traffic at a time when the community came alive in the criminal element.

While in the streets myself, it was an accepted and practiced *reality* wherein we left the daytime for the Square's, as we called them, but the night was ours. This was because our violent criminal behavior, in order to be practiced effectively, had to be cloaked by the darkness of night. I was keenly cognizant of the fact and was genuinely concerned about her safety and the perceived impropriety of a woman in traffic at night garnered. Though I was not comfortable with the fact that she'd be in traffic at times I thought were unsavory, she was a grown woman and the decision was ultimately hers.

She clearly expressed that the longevity of our relationship hinged on whether I could accept the fact that she would be more active and all that her being active implied. I didn't want to be without her and out of that fact, I conceded. She'd become the Head of a ladies' group in the Church which demanded her time and work. This fact procured resentment in me. I'd taken N'STEP® off of her plate in order to support her in her scholastic pursuit of her Ph.D. – and though this impeded the progress of N'STEP® - it was what a man did to support his woman.

Sacrifice of self was paramount to the growth of any relationship and I was not adverse to this fact, but to take on more work in the wake of my selfless sacrifice was disregarding and not congruent with our plan to build the N'STEP® brand – wherein we could effectuate change in our communities and simultaneously sustain and maintain oneself.

This had become a point of contention in our interaction. How could she not overstand the fact that N'STEP® and the resulting work in violence saturated communities as my salvation, my atonement my redemption, my destiny. This work was my life, and, in this work, I had life. There was no other reason for me to live! The God was only liberating me to do this work. I put this work on hold in order to assist you in your endeavor by creating a scenario that would afford you more time and space to actualize your pursuit, then you take on more work, that in essence, demands the very same time that I sacrificed.

This, to me, showed a lack of belief in my vision and a lack of faith in me. I did what I'd usually do in these situations. I went to my assigned cell, prostrated before The God, and after said prostration I got back to work on my book "Original Diamond Boy Part Two: The Transition."

"Perpetual Motion, Comrade! Against All Odds!" I thought out loud.

Chapter Thirty-Eight

I'd began taking a correspondence course in Physical Fitness & Nutrition in an attempt to gain certification in something that I enjoyed doing just in case I had to supplement my income upon my imminent liberation from my present circumstance. Also, in my attempt to get N'STEP® back on track by perpetuating my productivity, I contacted a woman named Rochelle who'd in prior years, acted as an advocate for my work.

Rochelle was an older woman who'd been active in poverty-stricken communities for years and had always believed in me and my work. She saw the necessity if N'STEP® and believed in the new paradigm and its transformational properties. She saw my vision clearly and was willing to invest her time and credentials in the furtherance of vison, and that was exactly what I needed at this point in my demonstration.

Rochelle had a beautiful spirit, but like most Afrikan American women. She had suffered emotionally from the trauma that deception and degradation spurns at the hands of Afrikan American boys masquerading as men. She was burdened and sometimes jaded in our rotation, but she had the presence of mind and character needed to ward off the stereotypes used to paint those incarcerated as unworthy of trust and unable to display moral rectitude. Rochelle began in earnest her advocation of N'STEP®, and the body of corpus that I'd produced facilitated her advocation.

I continued to work frenetically to ensure efficacious matriculation back into so-called free society upon release and on July 13, 2010, my concept "DIAMONDS IN THE ROUGH© (D.I.T.R.,pronounced "Deter), ENGAGING THE YOUTH, CHANGING THE FUTURE" became a registered trademark, and I was the owner of the Trademark.

Upon my request, Myisha had sent a copy of my children's book to our President, Barack Obama, as a gift of reverence for his Presidency. To my surprise, the President and First Lad of the United States of America sent a Thank You card bearing the seal of the United States Presidency. I was ecstatic.

I'd been having dreams that President Obama and myself were traversing inner city communities together, working on the issues that plagued these communities. Since he'd won the Presidency, I'd had three dreams that I conveyed to Myisha as visions of the President and myself working together – one being so vivid – that we sat at a Presidential table discussing my work in the community, with him offering me ideas to maximize the effectiveness of the work. These visions played in my mind on a continuum and served as inspiration to my day to day struggle for liberation.

Chapter Thirty-Nine

In late July 2010, the insidiousness of C/O Grime's surreptitious conspiracy to discredit my leadership among the Afrikan American population at CBCC became evident. Though I'd repelled his machinations through Misconduct Complaints in the past, this renewed slanderous advancement on his behalf would create a scenario that could potentially jeopardize the safety and security of the facility. C/O Grimes had been covertly feeding Judas' zealous ambition to be President of the CUO and he even went as far as to tender to Judas the CUO box that contained all documents pertinent to the function of the CUO.

A box that I'd been requesting as the President of the CUO for almost a year. The very same box that he'd told me in 2009 that he had no knowledge of its whereabouts and in 2010, in the presence of Xavier, Mr. Price, and Rasheed, stated that CUS Amplier had confiscated. This gave Judas, in my opinion, a sense of entitlement – a sense of exclusivity that fed not only his zealous ambition but also his ego. C/O Grimes then began to present me to Judas as a threat to his ambitions and to Afrikan American men's progress. C/O Grimes spoke of me as the reason that the CUO disintegrated, which was blatant fabrication.

What transpired, in reality, is that after I'd filed my complaint against C/O Grimes for the very same subversive tactics, he no longer wanted to sponsor the group – and by withdrawing his sponsorship – he, in effect, silenced our struggle. For without a sponsor, we could not hold meetings.

C/O Grimes manufactured a ploy to eliminate me as the President of the CUO, which automatically drew my opposition. My position was "In the absence of the President of the CUO, bylaws dictate that the Vice-President, which was myself, fill that vacant position." That was what I did and that's what I'd continue to do without reticence. C/O Grimes' ploy was to arbitrarily, through circumstance, erect Judas as the CUO President through his disparaging prevarications to Afrikan Americans about me and even going as far as to insinuate that if I would not relinquish the Presidency, he would not sponsor the CUO group.

I opposed his ploy vehemently, which resulted in the disdain of Judas. The stage for confrontation was set, all the actors cast, and the drama was prepared to unfold. One day, during a religious service on the chapel floor, it was 'Lights, Camera, Action!'. Judas approached me expressing the urgency of dialogue between us. I panned the room and saw that his forces we arrayed. Us being from opposite Structural Gang Cultures© exacerbated the ordeal. For when those loyal to me saw what potentially lie ahead, they arrayed themselves, dividing the room into two separate and distinct regiments.

Judas accused me of back-biting – and in light of my imminent liberation – being selfish in my staunch opposition to the premeditated move to co-opt the CUO. I knew that it was Judas' quest for clemency that motivated his desire to be the President of the CUO. His active involvement in groups would look good at his Clemency Hearing, but his reason was not born of integrity. It was born of selfishness. I couldn't, in good conscience, allow this to happen.

Yes, I was slated to be liberated, but I'd served the best interest of the Afrikan Americans in the Washington State Department of Corrections for the past 13 years – with integrity – and knowing Judas' reasoning made me uncomfortable with his aspirations.

"Brother, I'm packed", Judas said.

Informing me that he was reading, willing, and able to take this issue to its violent probability.

"Brother, I'm never unpacked", I returned his sentiment and panned the room. I saw the Gangster Disciples at the ready, but so were the Crips.

All that we'd worked to build would come crashing down at this moment, igniting a war between the Crips and the Gangster Disciples. A faction that I had the utmost respect for... This was the normal procession of the fabricated prevarications of C/O Grimes, who'd apparently reasoned that this would be the outcome of his skillful, insidious machinations. If it had not been for the intervention in our affairs by The God, this scenario would have ended in wanton bloodshed. But it didn't.

After returning to the module, Rasheed conveyed to me that I'd been greenlighted by the Gangster Disciples and that, in his perception, they'd come on that day to carry out the assault. An assault, he perceived to be sanctioned by Judas. I didn't want to believe Rasheed's assertion, but to be safe, I couldn't dismiss it. I immediately filed another Complaint against C/O Grimes.

Employee Misconduct Complaint:
Mrs. Diimmel (Assoc. Supt.) August 8, 2010

I am once again forced by the actions of your staff to seek redress though the administrative process in hopes of rectifying this very serious ad potentially disruptive flagrant breach of DOC Policies 800.010, 850.030, Department of Corrections Employee Handbook Code of Ethics & Expectations, and RCW's 42.20.080, 9A.12.080, 42.20.040 and 9A.80.010(1).

On or about 7-27-19 I spoke with C/O Grimes concerning a Complaint that I'd filed against him in June of 2009. Said conversation took place in the presence of Michael Harris, Rasheed Thomas, and Robert King in G-Unit. My complaint consisted of C/O Grimes informing Jamal Smith and Donald Betts, inaccurately, that my legally changed name was a STG name, and retaliatory behavior that he'd exhibited after said Complaint.

I then informed C/O Grimes that his negative depiction of two other offenders stemmed from said retaliatory motives and that his issuing of the CUO Box to another offender and attempt to circumvent the CUO Bylaws by disenfranchising those of us who were not unanimously elected by the body, was part and parcel of his ongoing animosity leveled at me for filing my Complaint in June of 2009.

C/O Grimes, after said conversation, went to A-Unit and again made false allegations concerning me and the CUO to at least (3) other offenders in his attempt to discredit me in my pursuit of the CUO's progress. (Said offenders will attest to the disparaging remarks C/O Grimes made about me. This prompted (3) offenders to approach me notifying me that C/O Grimes was in fact making statements to the effect of "Le'Taxione® is the reason that the CUO fell apart after Juneteenth, and he thinks he's going to be the President, but I've handled that already."

First and foremost, his statement that I was the reason that the CUO fell apart is "patently false" – violating RCW 9A.80.010(1) – depriving me of a lawful right or privilege under the color of the law. I have the right or privilege to move through this facility without fear of being targeted by staff whose disparaging remarks of an offender could result in a security issue – especially when he knowingly makes these false accusations in violation of RCW 42.20.040.

Said dissemination of this false information by C/O Grimes about me to other offenders in in violation of Policy 800.010 and 850.030 more particularly 800.010 IV (A) & (B).

The continued disparaging remarks made by C/O Grimes about me could procure a belief in Afrikan American offenders that if it wasn't for me, they would still have a CUO group, which could create a potentially hostile environment for me.

C/O Grimes must not be allowed to continue to fabricate and perpetuate this dissention between Afrikan American offenders – which is spurned by the Complaint that I was forced to file against him in June of 2009 due to his ignorance and misuse of authority. His actions are unethical, unprofessional, and criminal and should be measured by WAC 356-340010(1).

CC: Personal Files
Jeff Ellis – Attorney at Law

I couldn't believe the betrayal that lie at the gate of ambition mixed with selfishness, but I was real as penitentiary steel. Judas' words still ring in my ears. "Your struggle is not my struggle, Brother", he said.

But our camaraderie was built on the struggle for Afrikan Americans behind these steel curtains, but these facts are often subverted in one's unrighteous, "quest for relevance©." I continued to work on a CD with my celly to be released free of charge with my next book.

Perpetual Motion Comrade… Perpetual Motion.

Chapter Forty

On November 2, 2010, The Washington State Supreme Court Panel granted the State's motion for Discretionary Review. This meant that they would review the Appellate Court's decision to, in essence, liberate me. The state argued that the actual innocence doctrine that the Appellate Court applied to my appeal was incorrect. For though this doctrine had been used on a federal level, it had not been used on the state level; therefore, the application of the doctrine to my particular case was erroneous. Though, in fact, I was actually innocent of being a persistent offender (Three-Striker), they felt that I should not have access at this federal doctrine because I was a state prisoner, as if the federal courts had no jurisdiction over the state courts. Now that's erroneous. It is in fact the federal courts that interpret law after the state courts have ruled on the case.

Imagine a judicial system and officers of said system, even after realizing that a life sentence given to a man is invalid on it's face, continue to oppose correction of said sentence because as the dissent judge stated, "I agree that it is impossible to factually compare Le'Taxione®'s California conviction with a Washington State crime; but to say that he's actually innocent would invite a flurry of litigation (paraphrased)." The issue of others using this precedential ruling in my case to access justice (i.e. invite a flurry of litigation) should not be the issue at hand. The issue at hand should be that this man has received a life sentence unjustly, and courts being impartial fact finders, charged with the duty to administer justice, must correct this miscarriage of justice, for one's life hangs in the balance. The numbers of individuals that will access justice under the ruling in my case should be of no import, yet this is the very reason that my liberation was being delayed for the fact that "It is impossible to factually compare my California conviction with a Washington State crime" is the issue upon which my liberation was procured. The Washington State Supreme Court scheduled review of the Appellate Court's decision in my case and again, the waiting game was enacted.

Chapter Forty-One

Beyond the steel curtains of the Washington State Department of Corrections, the practiced ignorance that rationalized complacency and stagnation had become even greater than it had been in the past years. The envy of Judas had escalated to treachery unbeknownst to me, until I received public disclosure documents wherein he made a statement to C/O Cram concerning me that prompted the C/O to file a declaration in the Clallam County Superior Court against me – citing his fear and used my violent – but distant past confrontations with police and correctional officers to seek an injunction against me. Though Judas' statement was a blatant prevarication, he'd violated the cardinal prohibition against snitching and I received this news as an affront and a betrayal, that in my years of ignorance would have garnered the response that prison politics dictated and that was overwhelming, unmerciful violence.

But I stayed my hand. I no longer subscribed to the dictates of convicts, for I no longer considered myself a con. That aspect of my demonstration had long been eradicated and violence was reserved for self-defense, not self-imposition. Judas' envy had taken a life of its own. Envy has a natural aggressive progression which moves successively from envy to hate to murder. Envy, this "discontented desire for another's possessions or perceived advantages", is well documented throughout the scripture in the stories of Cain and Abel, Joseph and his brothers, and Saul and David to name a few. In every one of these stories, envy lead to a plot to murder the object of the enviers. The envy that Judas had for me would prove to be no exception.

It came to light that Judas had in fact made the statement concerning me to C/O Cram, a statement that C/O Cram attempted to use against me in our Clallam County Court hearing. This fact threatened his position amongst the Washington Gangster Disciples. He had to eliminate the source of information that depicted his lack of integrity and treachery. My cellie was too a Washington Gangster Disciple, so Judas approached him in the presence of the rest of the minions who were housed at the medium security building and offered them $350.00 to assault me – essentially greenlighting violence against me.

When this mandate against me was made evident to me through my cellie, I was amused. First of all, there was no one amongst those present that had the capacity or tenacity required to carry out an assault on me successfully because they were neither accustomed to or willing to go to the lengths that I was willing to go to I the defense of self.

During the time of this treachery, my Comrade, Charles Russell, had returned from the SHU back to general population. Brother Russell, as I called him, was a tried and tested soldier from Sand Diego, California. He was known for his violent exploits perpetuated against anyone who'd transgressed against him, including correctional officers. I remember when we were both house at the Monroe Correctional Complex when I heard C/O's radio sounding alarm that signified there was violence being perpetuated somewhere in the institution. As I watched C/O's dispatched to the disturbance in droves, I thought to myself "I hope that Brother Russell is not involved."

When it was all said and done, the word came back to me in the cell block that Brother Russell had successfully fended off the violent physical advance of several C/O's. I smiled out loud. Not that I condoned the violence, but I overstood one's need and right to defend oneself against malevolent advances.

Brother Russell as housed in the unit that I was in upon being placed in general population. Our camaraderie was natural, for we were both from California and kept our demonstration beyond reproach. I informed Brother Russell of the plot that had been hatched against me and his reaction was pure California.

Chapter Forty-Two

2011 had thus been a year of violence and betrayal. There had been two separate incidents wherein the Crips first battled the Pacific Islanders and then the Native Americans – so tensions were high and violence on the menu. In the midst of it all, this issue between Judas and myself threatened to escalate into yet another expressed form of genocide. It had the potential and propensity to procure a war between the factions that were both unwanted on my behalf and unnecessary. That being expressed, I refused to let anyone advance in a manner that would bring harm to my cipher – and if the attempt was made, I'd present a level of violence sure to act as a deterrent.

I made Brother Russell cognizant of the posture that I'd taken on this issue. His concern was that I not be involved in any activity that would affect my imminent release. Brother Russell's suggestion was that he act as mediator and if mediation didn't work, he would act in my stead to ensure that my liberation would not be jeopardized.

The next day at gym, Brother Russell presented the documented statement Judas made to C/O Cram against me, to one of the Gangsters Disciples and stated, "Here's the document. Le'Taxione® is going home and any attempt to impede him through any measure will be reciprocated in his absence." Days later the institution when on lockdown – confining everyone to their assigned cells due to the escalated violence – at which time – I was taken to the SHU under the auspices that I was active in the recent violence.

At this point, the reader must overstand that although I had nothing to do with the violence involving the Crips – I was a documented member of the Crips. The only way that I would be exempt from these kind of institutional sweeps was if I debriefed (meaning I would have to denounce the Diamond Crips and give the administration information concerning the status of members and their operation). In other words – I'd have become an informant. NEVER THAT!

While in the SHU, Judas was brought in and placed in the cell next to me. Considering the fact that he'd already furnished prevaricated information to staff about me, I saw this as the Administration's last-ditch attempt to implicate me in security threat group activity. I exhibited no mouth (said nothing to no one). In the silence of my assigned cell, I pondered the events that lead to my present circumstance. I replayed the betrayal and treachery.

I visualized those who'd feigned camaraderie but when they perceived conflict, took a position on the sidelines to watch as I prepared to engage a vast majority if opponents with very few allies. I vowed to disengage in any interaction with such cowardice upon release back to general population. Day 4 of being places in the SHU, Judas was transported out of the facility. His treachery had come back to him like a dog to his own vomit. His envy had engulfed him and the negativity that he'd emitted into the ethers had returned to him unabated – the earth is round. In February of 2011 my second children's book "A Bully's Behavior" was published.

Chapter Forty-Three

March 20, 2011, I spoke to my attorney, Jeff Ellis, and was made cognizant of the fact that on May 10, the Washington State Supreme Court would entertain the oral arguments of the State prosecutor and Jeff concerning my case. This news made me anxious – for I'd already won the case in the Appeals Court and the fact that the Supreme Court accepted the prosecutor's petition for discretionary review gave the Prosecutor one more opportunity to try and convince the courts that I should not have prevailed in my case.

The attempt would in all reality be an attempt to persuade the Supreme Court to discredit the Appeals Court finding, that my sentence be vacated, and I be remanded for sentencing wherein I could only be sentenced to 75 months. A fraction of the 14 years that I'd already served. That night, as I lay in the silence of my reality, I pondered the events that transpired during this 14-year ordeal and how they'd all shaped and fashioned me in one way or another.

What was seared into my conscious thought, as if branded into my mind as one would brand cattle, was the fact that I'd been deceived by the subtle sedition of one whom I'd believed to be my comrade in the struggle to elevate the consciousness of the brothers confined behind the steel curtains. And although his staff complicit plot to impede my demonstration disintegrated before his very eyes, this fact did not mitigate the reality of the attempt – which in turn frustrated my confidence in the prevalent mentality that permeated the Washington State Department of Corrections and the factions of the Structural Gang Culture© that nursed from the mammary gland of the system.

I do no propagate or condone violence in the perpetuation of oppression and or ignorance and recent history will testify to the fact that I, from behind the scenes of the Structural Gang Culture©'s prison politics, stopped activity that may have resulted in the death of several individuals on my distinct and separate occasions.

Not because I was active, but out of the respect that the factions had for my integrity in the peacemaking process didn't unveil this fact in an attempt to paint myself with the brush of sainthood, for I am far from that descriptive title, but I merely seek to make the reader conscious of the fact that individuals in an environment as depraved and dehumanizing as the prison industrial complex, hold in their very world, the power of life and death, necessitating the need for an avenue to true reform.

That being advanced, I could have submitted to my lower animalistic self and spoke in a manner that would have informed violence, but I chose peace, in hopes that the brothers self-accusing spirit would bear witness against him to the point where he atoned and sought forgiveness for his crime against his brother and the struggle. This dynamic which plagues every organization from government to the Structural Gang Culture© seldom ends with an acknowledgement or proclamation of wrongdoing – disallowing the redemption required to heal.

I'd recently received my physical fitness and nutritionist certification from the Stratton Institute, and I went to work on a children's self-help book for girls entitled "I Love Myself". I'd long ago come to the realization that though change comes from within, it is influenced from without. Armed with this fact, I continued to write and publish literature in so-called free society in hopes of imparting information that one could use in their developmental process in search of self.

I perceived a lack of self-worth, a distorted self-concept, which fed low self-esteem in girls and I attempted to address it. Contrary to popular positions, I couldn't adopt the posture of "as long as I affect one person..." I wanted to affect the masses! For it is the masses that suffer from poverty and destitution. It is the masses that come from fractured, impaired family structures. It is the masses that suffer from inequalities in health care and education. It's always the masses that suffer and I am one of the masses.

Chapter Forty-Four

On May 10, 2011 at 1:30 p.m., my case was again heard in the Washington State Supreme Court. Afterwards I spoke with Myisha who'd attended on my behalf. Myisha informed me that the hearing had in fact went extremely well and that the Supreme Court Justices had grilled the prosecuting attorney in an attempt to ascertain her legal position against my release which had been ordered by the Appellate Court. As always, the prosecutions' opposition to my release was weak, uninformed, and disintegrated in the midst of legal wrangling.

I'd planned to listen to the hearing via telephone as soon as Myisha had reached her home and when she had, I called again to do so. After listening to the hearing, I was again well pleased with my attorney's representation of me. Mr. Ellis was eloquent and very knowledgeable in his representation and aggressive – but tempered in his position. Myisha and I discussed the legalities of the hearing and also the impressions given to her by the Justices through the questions they'd published to both my attorney and the prosecution.

We'd always engaged in this legal discourse after litigation in my case and I revered the perspective she'd advance; her being an attorney. I was a layman to the law who'd been forced by circumstance to become a quasi-attorney in order to exact my liberation and I was good. It was I who had constructed the blueprint for my defense and advanced it to my attorney who saw the merit in my assertions and built a solid petition that would, four years later, secure my liberation. Myisha was a better legal mind than she would admit, and I learned from her through every legal discourse we'd engage in.

She was a human being that I could confide in when I'd grow weary of interacting with the prevalent, uncivilized behavior that was concomitant with the element of incarceration. She'd agreed that the hearing was favorable and reiterated the difference that the Supreme Court give to the Appellate Courts. We conversed for hours, listened to the video again, after which we said goodnight and returned to our respective realities – both longing for the same the… Justice!

Chapter Forty-Five

April 5, 2011 – my children's book "I Love Myself" went into publishing. In the interim I continued to construct the N'STEP® Gangology 101 correspondence course – that I may make accessible the curriculum to those confined behind the steel curtains of the American Prison Industrial Complex. I'd been contacted by sistas housed at the California Prison for Women in Chowchilla who's shown interest in my curriculum and wanted to further their knowledge of the psychological and sociological elements that cultivate and perpetuate gang violence.

The fact that I'd been awarded the National Community Service Award in January of 2011 for the work I'd been doing in the communities gave me extra publicity which procured extra responsibility. For some, according to the letters that I'd been receiving, I was the manifestation of reform and success. This fact was multiplied by my street credentials. I was tangible, accessible and had suffered from the very same experiences and mentality that plagued their rotation, but I'd – against all odds – transformed those trials, tribulations and traumas into something productive and they felt that if I'd done it, they too could do it – and they were right.

These letters that I would periodically receive were sobering. This is the same experience that I would have when I'd hear of

Tookie (RIP) and his struggle. Everyone, at times, needs to be able to look to someone else for direction, motivation, instruction, or inspiration. I came from the mud that they'd come from. They were flesh of my flesh. Cut from the same stone, facing the same obstacles, engaged in the same struggle, products of the same adversities. I owed them my life and was prepared to lay it down at their feet in our quest to ameliorate the seemingly inherent violence in our blighted communities across this wilderness called America.

Why did I owe them one might ask??? I owe them because I was one of the most significant advocates of the Structural Gang Culture© miscreant mentality, not because I was the hardest hoodsta on the planet, but because I was one of the most violent that could articulate and make attractive the Crip philosophy and ideology. This had been my major recruiting tool and I wielded it like a weapon. This would be the same tool I would employ in my attempt to significantly reduce gang violence.

There must be recompense for one's actions. No one on this Earth is without dirty hands and because the Earth is round, one gets out of the Universe what one puts into the Universe. So, it is incumbent upon us to right the wrongs that we advance in order to balance the scales of karma in our desire to experience the felicity inherent in The God's mercy and grace.

Chapter Forty-Six

I'd been in frequent contact with both Blue Bear and my daughter Mo'Nique. The gang violence in Fresno had spiked with random violence and indiscriminate gun play being the rule of the day. This mindless genocide had claimed the breath of children and this fact saddened Blue Bear. At times when we'd discourse, I could hear the malcontent in his voice as he recounted to me the heinous acts of aggression and their aftermath. The residual effects were always more devastating than the instant act. I could hear my comrade was growing weary and the intonation resonated in my psyche long after the discourse.

Mo'Nique, not living in West Fresno, had a more positive outlook, though she too was affected by the everyday hustle and bustle of life being in full session. She had tailored her activity in the community in a manner that paralleled and complemented my work. She was always a beacon of light and hope in the midst of gross darkness and ignorance. At times I'd be in awe of her for she came from me, one who was, at the time of her birth, so uncivilized and savage in my application of ideology and misogynistic in my perception of the feminine principle without a modicum of concern.

I'd call her on the phone. "Hi Daddy!" she would blurt out after the rigmarole of the recorded process.

"Hey baby girl!" I'd reply with as much if not more enthusiasm.

I marveled at the fact that she'd, in her developmental process, found a way to transcend my arbitrary absence and in her rotation and thanked God for her forgiveness. He belief in my work and unwavering support of the posture that I'd taken in this urgent dispensation of time was both significant and essential and her love for me, who'd been so far from home for so long, was an aspect of the force that compelled and propelled my ascension.

My grandson, Baby James, too inspired me, and I was proud of the fact that Mo'Nique had made his education a priority and demanded excellence of him. Mo'Nique and I planned to combine our talents upon my liberation in order to actualize our best opportunity for success in our endeavor to heal the community.

Blue Bear and I had already embarked upon this journey that had been predestined for us, resultant of the convulsions that our community was experiencing; a condition that we'd , in our immaturity and ignorance helped to perpetuate. This fact and the love that I had for the hood would cause my eyes to emit salty water in the silence of my assigned cell.

It would be easy for me, upon release, to get on some selfish me, me, me demonstration. In all reality, for the most part, I've had t transverse this sometimes unbearable circumstance by my lonesome, but I knew that my liberation was inextricably bound to an assignment that would place me back in the very same environment that I'd help taint. So, I assiduously employed my theory of selfish altruism that I may not only be an asset to the community at large, but I'd also be an asset to the community of self.

I'd weathered the enemy of youth… which is time, and came out on the other side more alive than dead, more anxious to rise above the stereotypical stigma that clings to each incarcerated human being like a symbiotic second flesh; a host of shame and marginalization, parasitic in its extraction of one's dignity and self-worth. I refused to capitulate under the relentless onslaught of negative images superimposed upon the psyche by environmental circumstances and individuals in concert with penological objection of dehumanization and degradation.

I resisted self-destructive impulses to regress in the midst of persistent injustice, starving my historical proclivity for violence while simultaneously feeding and nurturing the voice of God in me that we erroneously call our conscience; for whatever one feeds, grows, and whatever what one starves, dies.

Chapter Forty-Seven

August 2, 2001 started off like every other day behind the sullen gray walls of the prison industrial complex. I'd awakened at approximately 4:30 a.m., brushed my teeth, washed my face, prayed and turned the television to CNN to catch major corporation's interpretation of the news. The world was in convulsions in the midst of what was termed "Arab Spring". The U.S. had a 14 trillion-dollar debt and was facing default due to the posturing of the Republicans and weak resolve of the Democrats, seemingly to the elation of the tea party, a political powder keg with extremist elements.

I'd read a book back in 2002 by Walter Kaarp called "Indispensable Enemies" , wherein he dissects, with precision, the political theatre that I'd witnessed concerning President Obama's desire to raise the debt ceiling so that the country would not default on it's debts. I'd grown weary of this theatrical political wrangling and decided to write a letter to my mother, Mzazi.

Later on that day, I was made cognizant of the fact that the 9t Circuit Court, which governed the courts in the region wherein I was being held captive, had ruled that "actual innocence" could in fact be used as an exception to the time bar – which was the issue in my case under review by the Washington State Supreme Court. This

119

meant that there was now caselaw in this region, which supported what the Washington Appellate Court had already decided – resulting in my life sentence being vacated.

I was ecstatic. Now all the Washington State Supreme Court had to do was follow its governing court, the 9th Circuit. "It won't be long now" – I thought in silence while the plethora of issues within this concentration camp that procured tensions swirled beneath the surface of a labored conviviality. The prevalent sociogenic personality of the youth proved to disallow unity and fed the invidious distinctions that made us as unique as a people.

These invidious distinctions created and in-group and out-group by the insidious racism of those in authority. "It was only a matter of time before this circumstance became combustible", I thought, as I watched envy's aggressive nature progress and consume its hosts. Spontaneous combustion.

While on the yard, I was involved in an altercation that resulted in me having to be taken to medical and being stitched up. As I was escorted in handcuffs, my shirt crimson and saturated, I felt a peace that defied all logic. I was not angry, nor did I entertain the doctrine of retaliation© that I'd articulated and perpetuated with an iron fist when I was a servant to the miscreant aspect of the gang mentality©. Prison rules demanded that I retaliate and when one allows his environment to superimpose itself upon one's psyche, one becomes a product of his environment; but prison didn't create man. Man created prison from the dark recesses of his mind and just because on is physically confined, does not mean he must submit to the psychological capture that prison dictates. It would be easy for me to order the hit on my combatant – but no greenlight would be given, for this is were my cycle of violence has come full circle... and this is where I choose to end it.

Chapter Forty-Eight

It's been 34 days and I still languish in the SHU; 23 hours-a-day in an isolation cell – wherein I am allowed one hour out of said cell five days a week; but only three of those days, I'm allowed to take a 10-minute shower. At times I find myself captivated by the seemingly ubiquitous misery, pain, and psychosis of those whose intellect is too fickle to endure this satanic reality.

One brother on the cell had snapped, experiencing a psychological break from reality, and in this tier, he defecated into the food tray and when the C/O's came to collect the trays, he in a laissez faire manner, handed the tray out of his food slot to the C/O. It is not my intention by recounting this episode to offend the reader, but this is the reality of the sensory depravation that is concomitant with prolonged residence in intensive management unit cells; and the compounded inhumane treatment by those who have taken an oath to treat incarcerated persons with dignity and respect; yet use their authority to advance their malevolent ideology in an attempt to compensate for their inherent shortcomings and experiential emasculation.

This same brother recently tried what was perceived as a suicide attempt (at least that could have been the result of his actions). Now he languishes in the same cell with no water to drink or flush his toilet. He now has to ask the C/O's to flush his toilet after it has festered for days at a time – further subjecting himself to the whiles of those whose job, in its fundamental application, procures a loss of humanity, facilitating their soulless existence, in the only venue wherein they can experience even a semblance of liability.

And then there are those that the silence of a cell causes to chronically project, loquaciously, in an effort to deflect their mind's attempt to deem them culpable for their venality and insensate criminality. When one fosters antipathy for who and what he has become and the circumstance that this reality has placed him in, introspection becomes a self-inflicted gaping wound beyond the panaceatic properties of antibiotics oozing with every pulsation, the bile of psychological instability that perpetuates his psychosis, circumventing his need to discipline self. The stratum of this self-defeatist mentality being that of one can cast a light on another, it will allow him to continue his remiss fullness in self-evaluation. This, in turn, allows him to exercise escapism as it relates to the ineffable pain that plagues his self-negotiation and powerlessness. It is this lack of self-discipline that facilitates the prison experience and the absence of the knowledge of self that mandates it.

Chapter Forty-Nine

It is September 19, 2011 and I can hear the guy up on the tier that defecated in his food tray attempting to engage a C/O in extra curricular conversation. Like a child trying to garner the attention of a parent and I prognosticate that just as when all positive attempts by the child are ignored, negative attempts will be sure to follow. He's now got the attention of the Sergeant. At last he commands the interaction that he so craves. All morning he's been casting profligate sentences out into the tier, as a fly fisherman casts his rod, in an attempt to get one to bite, take the bait and engage him in frivolous discourse. To no avail, I can hear him lamenting the Sergeant that the vents in the assigned cell are not working correctly, the input and output dysfunctional. With the turn of a dial, the Sergeant assures him with brevity that all systems are go. This interaction was too brief, too matter of fact to garner satisfaction for the complainant.

The Sergeant exits to finish his rounds. A moment of silence, then the cascading sound of water rush over the top tier to the bottom tier. As I presciently noted, the negative attempt to garner attention becomes manifest. The silence of a cell has again become unbearable and the occupant had flooded his cell by obstructing the designed path of the water in his toilet forcing it to overflow onto the tier. This event interrupted the monotony of the SHU.

It ironically became entertainment for that moment, in that moment, it relieved the tier of serious thought, blurred the lines of prison politics. Now I hear the chronically projective, loquacious one who lies content and wallows in the littered fields of his own psychosis attempting to pontificate and rationalize the uncivilized act of flooding one's assigned cell as a noble act congruent with struggle. "How dare he", my subconscious screams into my conscious mind.

One who has arbitrarily adopted the miscreance that he deems to be a Black cultural norm due to it commercialization – a constructed fad in his plight of escapism and self-denial, attempts to superimpose his phantasmagorically romanticized oversimplification of what struggle is and espouses this ruse as if it was grounded in Black political ideology. One who has not adorned the attire of Black skin in this environment – who has not breathed through Black nostrils the atmosphere of this social-order – one who has not heard the degradation thought Black ears concerning his lot in life. As if his adoption of slang or perceived Black vernacular, connotations and intonation, affords passport. How paternalistic - his premature verbal ejaculations.

One must engage and endure one's own internal struggle and maintain clarity of purpose before one can pontificate and convey through correlation the principles of struggle. Anything less is disingenuous, merely putrid verbal flatuations.

The tier falls silent.

I hear footsteps and keys jingling. The C/O's cuff the complainant without incident – he complies. They transfer him to another module. The process will start over again in earnest as soon as he's ignored, and he doesn't receive the attention that the silence of a cell causes him to crave.

EPILOGUE

I finished this memoir in solitary confinement (SHU) amidst the madness concomitant with being caged like an animal, subjected to sensory deprivation and deprived of intimate human contact and/ or interaction. I was asked by a brother on the tier who I'd admonished for allowing this synthetic environment to turn him into itself – "How can you continue to stay positive surrounded by all this chaos?"

"I extract peace from the midst of chaos", I answered.

As I sat back at my desk, I pondered the answer I'd given the brother. It was true. I'd grown accustomed to extracting peace from the midst of chaos. As a matter of fact, I'd been most productive in the midst of in here chaos that is concomitant with the element of incarceration – and this realization procured in me pause. The prison environment affects many people in various ways – but it affects everyone who drinks from this trough…everyone.

It is so oppressive, degrading, and dehumanizing that one finds himself in a perpetual struggle to retain his humanity and his civility – for the rule of this environment is animalistic and violence is always on the menu. For this is the result of injustice veiled in a pretty package called the penological objective and though it is dispensed to every ethnicity, Black men receive the lion's share – which in turn affects their psyche to the point where they internalize through introjective projection and turn in on self and kind.

They become what they've been erroneously labeled and act out of the self-fulfilling prophecy of self-annihilation with wanton vigor. Clayton A. Hartjen – in the book "Crime and Criminalization", states: "Insofar as the criteria for labeling someone a criminal reflects some disparity in group interests and power, that which is defined as crime and those who are selected to fill the criminal status are socially created objects of the structural characteristics of human society that produce conflict and an inequitable distribution of power in society."

When one accepts and internalizes negative stereotypes about himself and his culture, he acts on impulse driven by internalized rage for his status in society and ultimately, he acts against his own self-interests to the perpetuation of the negative stereotypes. They become complicit in their own negation. Though there is a clandestine, insidious hand that set in motion the circumstances that Black men find themselves in today, I ask, who is it that is disproportionately killing Black men?

Always take into account the Judas factor.
Sanitize your cipher.
In Solidarity,

Le'Taxione®

Lightning Source UK Ltd.
Milton Keynes UK
UKHW02063506S0820
367798UK00011B/938